LETTERING AND DESIGN

LETTERING AND DESIGN

Practical Uses For Your Handwriting

·Carole Vincent·

BLANDFORD PRESS

POOLE · NEW YORK · SYDNEY

First published in the UK 1986 by Blandford Press,
Link House, West Street, Poole, Dorset BH15 1LL

Distributed in the United States by Sterling Publishing Co, Inc, 2 Park Avenue, New York, NY 10016

Distributed in Australia by Capricorn Link (Australia) Pty Ltd PO Box 665, Lane Cove, NSW 2066

British Library Cataloguing in Publication Data

Vincent, Carole
 Lettering and design: practical uses for your
 handwriting.
 1. Lettering
 I. Title
 741.6′1   NK3600

ISBN 0 7137 1638 X

Typeset by August Filmsetting, Haydock, St. Helens
Printed in Great Britain by R. J. Acford Ltd., Chichester, Sussex

Contents

Acknowledgements

The author and publishers wish to thank the following for permission to include their writing and illustrations in this book:

Jacqueline Allan   Katy Barrell
Geoffrey Bayfield   Thelma Beswick
John Beswick   Muriel Blackett
Pamela Bousfield   Nicholas Colwill
Joan Carrigan Cork   Lisa Cronin
Elisabeth Davey   Cynthia Deacon
Mary Edward-Collins   Philippa Edwards
Ann Fletcher   Harriet Halstead
Andrew Hobbs   Lilian Holborow
Jacqueline Jarvis   Helen Lawrence
Susanna Mount   Glen Mulcahy
Dorothea Pattinson   Ronald Pearson
Sharon Power   Joanna Tague
Rosalind Thomas   Ivan Upright
Paul Wadey   Katy Zoeftig
Sarah Zoeftig

and also Wendy Selby, S.S.I. for the final page and an expert calligrapher's advice on the manuscript.

The photographs are by John Beswick.

The author would also like to thank A. Mary Shaw for corrections to the manuscript, Cleo Murch for typing it, John and Julia Burns for the use of their photocopying machine, Felicity Carter of her publishers, and many friends and students for advice and encouragement.

Introduction

Good handwriting has a uniformity and rhythmic flow that is constant. Essentially it must be legible, a reasonable size with well-formed letters and have good spacing between words and lines of writing. It is a matter of pride in the way you present yourself, a courtesy to those who are intended to read it and a skill which, when done well, is a pleasure to both.

A personal style of lettering can be developed from good handwriting and for many people may be achieved more quickly than by abandoning a style that has been used for years to learn a recognised formal style.

Designing with your lettering is fun. You could make your own greetings cards and invitations, design a 'house-label' for home-made wines and preserves, produce posters, your own brochure or magazine or just enjoy, for its own sake, producing a page of beautiful writing.

- Does your handwriting give a good impression? Would it help you to pass an examination, to gain a place at college or secure a top position?
- Or, do your family and friends complain about your untidy and illegible handwriting?
- Is it daunting to think of learning a new style?
- Would you like to develop a personal form of lettering?
- Good design is an important part of communication. Would you like to learn how to lay out a page of writing?

Lettering and Design – Practical Uses for Your Handwriting is a realistic approach to these problems. The illustrations for the book were provided by over thirty people who represented a wide variety of ages, styles and competence. I hope that the examples of their struggles and achievements will encourage you to improve your own writing and find that doing this is a pleasurable and rewarding experience.

Carole Vincent
Boscastle, 1986.

Marie Dewar,
Maxwell Farm House,
Bencubbin,
Launceston.

7. XII. 84.

Dear Brigid

Thank you for your invitation to visit you and your family next week-end. I would be delighted.

On Friday I shall travel by Jay's coach to Plymouth and another coach from there to Weymouth. I should be with you at approximately 4.30 p.m.

I look forward to seeing you all.

much love
Marie.

356, Sioux Avenue,
Richmond,
Virginia,
U.S.A. 23226
9ª December, 1984

My dear Kaye

Thank you so much for my birthday present — it was good of you to remember the day! And it was good of you to choose a Dylan Thomas I haven't read.

Incidentally we studied Dylan Thomas at Biddy's literature class last year, but it was mostly his poetry and very little of his prose. This book looks to be a good mixture of both.

Again, thank you for your thought.

Love,
Muriel.

Peel's Cottage
Windham
Kendal
Cumberland

3rd Dec.

Dear John,

Having returned safely to the sticks I felt I must put pen to paper to say what a pleasure it was to see you again after so many years. Your choice of restaurant was as always superb. I am not sure we shall be able to compete when you came down in May.

I have contacted Bill and Peter and they both will be able to come down during your stay.

Yours as ever
Godfrey.

Trevean
Trevenning
St Tudy

3rd December

Dear Fiona,

Thank you for ringing me last night.

I shall arrive at Paddington on Sunday.

Could you please ask the boys what they would like for Christmas and let me know when I see you.

I am so looking forward to seeing you all again.

Love from.
Mary.

Letters written before any instruction in improving handwriting or layout was given.

Part One

Improving your Handwriting

The correct pen hold and position of the
paper for a right-hander.

Until the age of fourteen I wrote using Marion Richardson based letters, although they never really joined up properly:

The smell of old crayon engulfed the air in the tiny wooden hut. Seven small children

My first encounter with handwriting

I was taught to write by a Canadian whose style was the

I am left handed, I was very bad at spelling. I learnt to write with my left hand tied behind me.

When at school I spent innumerable hours in the practice of 'Pot-hooks.'

I remember being given a lesson on hand-writing when I was about nine years old.

Handwriting education at secondary school is non-existent, but at primary school we were taught

When I was at Primary school, not only did we have to learn printed writing, but later joined-up writing.

It's a very long time ago, but I fancy that learning to write must have been a happy experience — I well remember the joy of being allowed to use INK!

Part One

Improving your Handwriting

Handwriting is a craft practised by nearly everyone. It is a visual expression of speech and a means by which we deliberately set down messages we want to communicate. Good handwriting is essential to present your message with maximum impact. It is a skill which can be appreciated by both writer and reader.

At first there will be no attempt to make you change the character of your handwriting, only suggestions for ways to improve legibility and personal style, without loss of speed. These will be followed by a consideration of the layout on the page. Think of the many situations for which you need good handwriting: writing letters, cards, informal invitations, essays, reports, notes, writing cheques and filling in forms.

Before you start the process of analysing your writing you must provide yourself with several examples so that you can compare them with the improved versions that should follow. You will need to collect a few things together:

- Writing paper and an envelope.
- Post card or birthday card.
- A blank cheque.
- An official form.
- Plenty of plain or ruled file paper.
- Tracing paper or very thin typing paper or greaseproof paper.
- A pen, ruler and pencil.

Make sure that you are well organised and sitting comfortably at a desk or a table before you begin.

A random sample of handwriting from students in the classes before any tuition was given.

Write a short letter of one or two paragraphs, address the envelope, write the postcard or birthday card, fill in the cheque and the form. Put these on one side as you will need them later.

Most people have two or three sorts of handwriting. One for scribbling notes, a personal shorthand not intended for anyone else to read. Another, everyday writing, used for long letters and essays, which needs to be legible but done quickly, and a third which is used for special communications. The first two are derived from the third and it is the third we shall analyse, hoping that the second will improve as a consequence.

In your best handwriting, write about three lines: your name, where you live, what you are doing or thinking, what you remember about being taught to write. It does not matter what you write as long as it is three lines of continuous script. Now look at it.

- Is your writing easy to read or not?
- Does your writing look attractive or is it an untidy scrawl?
- Does it take you a long time to write neatly?
- Do you find the physical effort of writing tiring? Does it produce back-ache, handache or a headache?

Legibility
Legibility matters most. This depends on the size of the writing, the space between words and between lines of words, the consistency of the slope of the writing, as well as the formation of individual letters.

First, consider the *size* of your writing.
Is it too small for most people to read easily? You may have good eyesight and feel it really should not matter, but think of those having to read it.

This writing is too small for most people to read easily, and is a result of narrow lined paper, supplied at schools.

Next, count the number of *words per line*. An average of ten or eleven is sufficient for your reader to read fluently. Over that number it is difficult to read in phrases or sentences.

Is your writing so large that it appears clumsy and allows too few words on each line? At school you have to conform to the line spacing in exercise books which is generally 8 mm ($\frac{5}{16}$ in). If you have to do much writing on lined paper you need to adapt your writing to the spacing provided. Using unlined paper, you can space your lines to suit the size of letters natural to you.

My writing is too large for the lines in school exercise books.

Check the *spacing* of your lines of writing by drawing a line in between.

I remember being given a lesson on hand writing when I was about nine years old. I was given a white Italic pen + a book to copy

When I was at Primary school, not only did we have to learn printed writing, but later joined-up writing. We used to write endless rows of the alphabet, with all letters joined.

Do the descenders (the downstrokes of letters like f, g, j, p, q, y) overlap the ascenders (the upstrokes of letters like b, d, h, k, l, t) and the capital letters of the line below? Your writing will be easier to read if there is a clear division between one line and the next. It may be that you have developed unnecessary flourishes on ascenders and descenders and not that your writing is too large.

Stage one is to make sure that there is a clear division between one line of writing and the next. This you can do by reducing the overall size of your writing, controlling the flourishes on ascenders and descenders or increasing the width between the lines of writing.

If you, or others, feel that your writing is too small, then make it larger!

I remember being given a lesson on handwriting when I was about nine years old. I was given a white Italic pen and a book to copy from.

When I was at Primary School, not only did we have to learn printed writing, but later joined-up writing

Next, look at the spacing between words. How many times can you write the letter 'o' between each word?

Havingooooattendedooomanyooschools, ooohave neverooadoptedogoao haveoobeenotaughtoo a specificooostyleoo dfooowritingo theo aboveoois

Handwritingoeducahouoatoesecondaryoschoolouonon-existent, obutoatoprimaryoschooloweowereotaught theobasics – spacingoofo lettersoandobetweenowords,

If there is more than one letter 'o' or insufficient room in between to write even one letter 'o', then you should consider the spacing of your words. If the gap is too large the reader has to hop from one word to the next and he is unable to read fluently. This also means that you cannot write fluently. Closer spacing will speed up your writing and it will look better.

If the space between words is too small or words are linked from one word to the next, this too makes difficulties for the reader.

Stage two, then, is to be consistent in the spacing of your words and this space should be about the size of one letter 'o'.

Having•attended•many•schools,•I•have•never•adopted,•or•have been taught a specific style of writing. The above is a sample of writing that I have imitated and can change at will

Handwriting•education•at•secondary•school•is•non-existent, but at primary school we were taught the basics - spacing of letters and between words,

Now, consider the *uniformity* of your writing. Use a pencil to draw lines through the stems and the upright parts of your letters.

At the age of thirteen I went through several changes of handwriting; it was fashionable! I practiced different styles

When I was at primary school, not only did we have to learn printed writing, but later joined-up writing.

It's a very long time ago, but I fancy that learning to write must have been a

Are these uprights parallel or not? They should be if you want to improve the look and the legibility of your writing, and it is essential that they are parallel before making a start in lettering.

If they are parallel, is the slope forward, upright or backwards? Some people say that *backward*-sloping writing is a sign of bad character. The reason it is not accepted by calligraphers is both visual and psychological. We write and read from left to right and a backward-sloping writing therefore goes against the forward trend. This is a common fault in left-handed writers who were badly taught or have acquired bad habits to enable them to avoid smudging what they have written. Writing which has a pronounced *forward* trend, on the other hand, can be difficult to read. To be easily read, your writing should be upright or gently sloping forward.

If the stems and upright parts of your letters vary from sloping backwards to

The correct pen hold and position of the paper for a left-hander.

16

vertical or sloping forward then the problem is fundamental. Good, even hand-writing depends upon holding the pen correctly, having the paper in the right position on the desk and sitting properly to write. Check these now and at intervals later on. Frequent correction is needed to break bad habits.

Many difficulties in writing are caused by holding the pen incorrectly. The pen should be held between the thumb and forefinger, with the forefinger slightly on top and the middle finger supporting the pen underneath. The fourth and little fingers should be tucked underneath to continue the support along the

A comfortable sitting position for writing.

side of the hand to the wrist. The shaft of the pen should rest lightly between the junction of the thumb and index finger and point over the right shoulder for a right-handed person and slightly to the left of the left shoulder for a left-handed person.

Make sure that you have the correct fingers and thumb holding the pen and that you are not gripping the pen too tightly. Your hand should move easily across the page.

Where is the paper in relation to your body?
If you are right-handed the left-hand side of the page should be opposite your middle. If it is any further to the left there is a tendency to write in an arc. It is easier to maintain consistency with the paper square to your body. If you are left-handed the paper should be at an angle with the right-hand bottom corner down, opposite the middle of your body and slightly further away than would be comfortable for a right-hander. Wrong positioning of the paper causes many difficulties for a left-hander. Extraordinary ways of holding the pen are adopted to compensate in order to see what is being written and to prevent smudging. I have seen this happen when a right-hander and a left-hander shared a double desk and had their writing hands on the inside! A left-hander would find it much easier to write from right to left but, as this cannot be, time and effort should be spent to find the most comfortable position for writing. However, when the left-hander attempts lettering on a large scale he or she will have to adapt to the paper being square to the body.

Equally important at all times is the way in which you sit to write. If the desk or table is too high or too low for you to sit with a relaxed but straight back, then your writing will suffer. Your feet should rest comfortably on the floor and not be twisted around the chair legs. Use a foot-stool if your chair is too high. It is easier to write with the desk or table top raised at an angle of 20°–30°. If the top is fixed, you can use a drawing board supported on a block of wood, or resting in your lap and supported by the edge of the table.

When you are sitting comfortably, the paper in the right position, the pen held correctly, try writing those three lines again. Is the slope of your writing more consistent? It should be. However, if the stems are still not parallel examine this further possibility.

The action of writing comes not only from the fingers but also from the easy movement across the page of the whole hand and the arm. It may be that you

are keeping the side of the hand fixed on the paper so that your writing is
formed in an arc, or you could be keeping your elbow firmly tucked in to the
side of the body. Try a few lines of continuous scribble to see if you can loosen
up and gain freer movement across the page.

At the age of thirteen I went through several
changes of handwriting, it was fashionable.

When I was at Primary School. not only did we
have to learn printed writing . but later joined . up

It's a very long time ago, but I fancy that learning
to write must have been a happy experience ~

If you intend doing no more than improve your ordinary writing you may feel
that too much stress is being put on the evenness of the slope. However, if you
want to progress to a more formal script and lettering, uniformity is essential.

Lastly, how clear and well-formed are the individual letters in your writing? At
this stage it is legibility and not style that matters. Most of us have certain
letters in our handwriting that are badly formed, exaggerated or diminished

ABCDEFGHIJKLMNOPQRSTUVWXYZ
abcdefgkijkluNopqrstuvwxyz
M M M M   b h m p r v   b h m p r v

ABCDEFGHIJKLMNOPQRSTUVWXYZ
abcdefghikjlmnopqrstuvwxyz
hhhh   mmmmm   nnnnn   uuuuu   vvvvv

and often unrecognisable. The letters 'r' 'h' 'm' 'n' 'u' in lower case (small letters) often become flattened into an illegible scribble. Look at these letters in your writing and at any others which are badly formed; write them out several times, improving their shape.

Another common fault is exaggerated or diminished ascenders and descenders. You may have realised this problem when you checked the spacing between your lines of writing. Overlapping ascenders and descenders can make your writing illegible but if they are too short it may be difficult to distinguish an 'a' from a 'd' or a 'g'.

a b c d e f g h i j k l m n o p q r s t
u v w x y z 3

a b c d e f g h i j k l m n o p q r s t
u v w x y z

a b c d e f g h i j k l m n o p q r s
t u v w x y z

b d f g h j k l p q t y b d f g h l k j l

Those of you who have loops on certain letters should make sure that these loops are slender. They can deteriorate into ovals, or even circles, which is both ugly and confusing.

The smell of old crayon engulfed the air in the tiny wooden hut. Seven small children

The smell of old crayon engulfed the air in the tiny wooden hut. Seven small children

Inconsistency in the size of letters or the spaces between them in any one word will also make your writing difficult to read. Slight variations are acceptable; your writing need not be as mechanical as that from a typewriter but exaggeration can make reading difficult.

How do you join letters together and dot the 'i' and cross the 't'? In an italic-based hand certain letters are better not joined and attempts to do so often cause illegibility. Capitals, on the whole, should not be joined. In basic copper-plate writing the continuity of the script is maintained by the flowing joins of one letter into the next. If this is your style, make sure the joins are not exaggerated. Dotting an 'i' and crossing a 't' is often an afterthought and misplaced or extended. Check that yours are not obtrusive.

I was taught to write by a Canadian whose style was the typical North American slant.

I was taught to write by a Canadian whose style was the typical North American slant.

Some people deliberately misform letters or words to cover up bad spelling. Think positively! If you improve the shapes of your letters perhaps better spelling will follow.

Rewrite the three lines you wrote at the beginning. There should be evidence of a considerable improvement. It may take you longer and your style may be upset temporarily but your writing should be legible.

Speed and Effort
In the early stages of improving your handwriting you are bound to feel that you have sacrificed speed in order to write more clearly. However, for most of us there are times when we need to write quickly and it would be a pity if you felt the time spent improving legibility was wasted. If an essay, report or long letter is difficult to read it will not receive the attention you expect. The reader will skip through the pages of writing or struggle through, trying to decipher

based letters, at... fourteen I wrote using Marion Richardson

The smell of crayon engulfed the air in the tiny wooden Hut.
...ren each clasped a fat colourful crayon with

My first encounter with handwriting was

I wa... ght to write by a Canadian
Canad... was the typical... Ink

I am left-handed, I was very bad at
at spelling...arnt to write with my left
hand tied behind me.

When at ... School I spent innumerable
in the p... the practice of 'Pot-hooks.'

I remember...being given a lesson on handwriting
writing whe...about nine years old.

Handwritin...education at secondary school is non-
existent, b...at primary school we were taught

When I wa...at Primary School, not only did we
learn printed...printed writing, but later joined-

It's a...ng time ago, but I fancy that learning
that learn...t have been a happy experience — I
happy exp...the joy of being allowed to use INK!

The handwriting of the students, who provided the first sample, after correcting the inconsistencies in their writing.

individual words, making it easy to lose the sense of what has been said. It creates a situation that is similar to a child learning to read word by word or even letter by letter instead of by phrases, sentences or paragraphs.

- Use the three lines you wrote at the beginning and repeat them if necessary.
- Write as much as you can in one minute exactly. Try again, but this time in your best handwriting.

I remember learning to write at kindergarten when I was only 4 yrs old. We used to have small exercise books where we practised rows & rows of letters — I used to enjoy the patterns these made.

I remember learning to write at kindergarten when I was only 4   *(47 words in 1 minute)*

I remember learning to write at kindergarten when I was only four years old. We had small exercise books where we practised   *(22 words in 1 minute)*

- How many words per minute did you write in the first attempt and how many in the second?
- Was there much difference in the number of words and how do they compare for legibility?

Like this I write 40 words a minute

Writing like this, I write 16 words per minute,

I am left handed and like this can write 52 words a minute

Writing like this I can do 42 words in a minute.

Writing like this I can do 21 words in a minute.

I can write 23 words like this in one minute

These examples show a variation in speed of writing from over forty to under twenty words a minute. There are about four hundred words per page of ruled A4 file paper, using average sized writing. At a rate of twenty words per minute you could write only nine pages in three hours, whereas at forty words per minute you would write eighteen pages. If you are a student you may feel that it is necessary to increase your speed of writing. How can you write more quickly and maintain legibility? The way you sit, hold your pen, and position the paper should be right. Writing that is too large, with exaggerated ascenders and descenders, as well as large gaps between words, will slow you down but, more importantly, there should be an easy flow and rhythm in your writing. If there are many letters in your words that are not joined, the rhythm will be jerky. You may have learned a style that did not encourage joining letters in words or adopted it to improve legibility. However, if speed is important, a compromise is necessary. Practise writing patterns and rows of joined letters to obtain a continuous rhythm.

Writing like this I write 21 words a minute.
uuuu mmm wwww huhuhu cacaca eeeee

What do you use to write with when speed is essential? Try using a biro, a felt or fibre-tipped pen, and a fountain pen. Probably, using a biro is the quickest, but what does it do to your writing? Biros are one of the main causes of unattractive and illegible handwriting. The hand slips lightly across the page in an uncontrolled manner or, to avoid this, it is tightly gripped and engraved into the paper. Try gripping your pen tightly and feel what happens. Tension in the fingers is transferred to the hand, arm and neck and this can be a cause of headaches when writing for a long time.

A fountain pen has a more flexible nib and seems to induce an easy rhythm and flow in your writing. In time and with practice it can be used as quickly as a biro or fibre pen, with a more attractive and legible result.

Now, paying attention to the way you sit, hold your pen, and to word and line spacing as well as the flow of your writing, time yourself for a minute to see if there is an improvement in the number of words written without loss of legibility.

Joining the letters improves the speed to 42 words a minute.

Style

Beautiful handwriting has a uniformity and rhythmic flow that is constant. Essentially it must contain all the factors required for legibility: a reasonable size and formation of letters, good spacing between words and lines with a consistency of slope and flow in the writing. Individuality and character in handwriting does not mean developing idiosyncracies in style or flamboyance in letter formations, nor does it mean producing a style that is not immediately recognisable as your own. Even if we were all taught the same way, it would not be long before individual characteristics showed themselves. In fact, all of us will have been taught one of two basic styles of writing and both were derived from the same source, the Latin or Roman alphabet.

The two basic styles are *italic* and *copperplate*, although there are many styles or variations of these which have become accepted methods in their own right.

Copperplate writing uses loops for joining and some letters such as E F G and I are different from those normally found in print.

Italic-based writing has no loops and some letters are not joined. It may be angular or even spiky but often it is more rounded.

Look at your writing and try to decide which style you learned. If you use loops for joining, and some capitals such as 'E', 'F', 'G' and 'T' are different from those normally found in print, then it is likely you were taught copperplate. If your writing is angular or spiky with no loops and several letters unjoined you may have been taught italic. If it is more rounded and flowing without loops you probably were taught one of the modified forms of italic, such as that of Marion Richardson.

These students learned italic or one of the modified forms of italic, such as Marion Richardson.

Until the age of fourteen I wrote using Marion Richardson based letters, I was not taught to loop my letters. My writing is italic based. A simple rounded writing is easier for a left hander I remember being taught nice rounded letters.

Exaggerated loops can make ones writing illegible.

Copperplate handwriting should always look elegant.

'Pot-hook' practice was basic to Copperplate.

These students were taught copperplate writing.

It is not always easy to tell as most of us pick up characteristics from parents and teachers and incorporate them in our own style. Similarities in style within a family are an interesting observation. Sometime, look at examples of the handwriting of parents, grandparents, brothers and sisters to see if you were influenced by any of them.

The author's grandfather, father and herself have many similarities in style.

Do you want to change your style of writing? The work you have done so far will have modified your writing. If it looks well you can use this as a basis for the lettering and design work which follows. The analysis and practice of individual letters you will do in Part 2 will help to improve their shape and uniformity without imposing a recognisable formal style. However, you may decide that now is the time to learn italic or copperplate writing, in which case I suggest you work from a book that deals only with one kind of writing before you continue with the lettering and design work which follow. But for many of you the changes in your style will not be so drastic. To abandon the style you have used for years and adopt a new one takes a great deal of practice and determination.

26

You could make some changes other than the improvements already mentioned which would make your writing more attractive.

- You might change the slope from upright to sloping forwards or vice versa.
- You could change the length of ascenders and descenders but take care that they are not excessive nor so small that it is difficult to distinguish an 'a' from a 'd'.
- The change that will affect you most is the pen you use for writing. There is little hope of producing beautiful handwriting without a good pen. The right pen for you becomes part of your hand when you write. It should be the right size for you to hold, the shaft should fit comfortably in your hand and the nib should be the right thickness for your letters and, above all, it should be easy to use. A biro or fibre-tip pen will never be as personal as your own fountain pen. Resolve now always to use a fountain pen when you want to write well, you may surprise yourself by the improvement in your writing.

I pick up a biro and write
all upright and tall
fine felt pens produce
a more dashing slope
with longer descenders
GOSH WOTS THIS!
Gosh sorry Carole ~
I should be writing
with my best italic pen.

This is a medium fine Italic nib.

This is an old Onoto Swan pen

Round hand pen makes the writing sit upright

very fine and soft fibre tip for ease

even finer fibre tip, fast and smooth

fountain pen with rounded nib

my favourite fountain pen.

Pens and Paper

There are many good pens on the market and the better shops will allow you to try out several nibs to find the one that suits you.

Modern fountain pen with soft, rounded nib.

Traditional fountain pen with more flexible, soft rounded nib.

Chisel-shaped italic nib suitable for right-handers.

Left oblique italic nib suitable for left-handers.

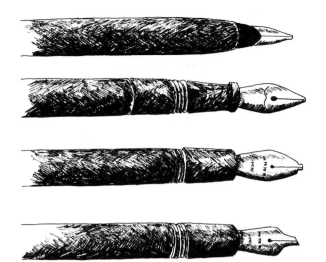

Basically, you need to decide whether you will use a rounded, soft nib or a chisel-shaped nib. Much depends upon the situation and, personally, I use both – the soft, rounded nib for everyday use, such as writing letters, cheques and notes, and the chisel-shaped italic nibs for formal writing. The size of the italic nib depends upon the size of your writing, hence it is wise to buy a pen with screw-in nibs in a range of fine, medium and broad, to B2, B3 and B4 suitable for lettering. These can be bought in sets. If you are left-handed you will need oblique nibs. These screw-in nibs can be and should be replaced at intervals. After much writing they may become soft or distorted and you will lose the sharp lines the nib produces. Another decision is whether to use black or blue ink and whether this should be supplied in cartridge form or the pen filled from a bottle of ink. The former is obviously more practical if your writing is done in several places. Indian ink should not be used in a fountain pen but if you use it for lettering purposes then wash the pen immediately afterwards.

Finally, think about the paper you use. It will vary in size and weight according to the situation but it must be smooth and of good quality. In letter writing the trend towards laid paper (ribbed, textured paper) will suit a typist but it is a difficult surface to use for handwriting.

Do not write on a block of paper as you cannot support your hand at the bottom of the page. At the other extreme, one piece of paper on a hard surface is not suitable. Thick card, or blotting paper on your desk or table top is a satisfactory solution.

These four students changed their style of writing during the course.

Having attended many schools, I have never adopted, or have been taught a specific style of writing.

Having attended many schools, I have never adopted, or have been taught a specific style of writing. The above is a sample

The smell of old crayon engulfed the air in the tiny wooden hut. Seven small childen each clasped a fat colourful crayon with tiny tense fingers.

The smell of old crayon engulfed the air in the tiny wooden Hut. Seven small children each clasped a fat colourful crayon with tiny tense fingers. Our first writing lesson had begun.

I remember having to do 'joined-up-writing' at primary school. Line after line of supposedly flowing letters.

I remember having to do 'joined-up-writing' at primary school. Line after line of supposedly flowing letters.

Learning to write is now only a foggy memory. Pencils without points, acres of dog eared copy books—

Learning to write is now only a foggy memory Pencils without points, acres of dog eared copy books.

Page Layout

Now, consider the way you set out a page of writing. We all know people whose writing looks superb on a page and yet it is difficult to read, and others whose writing is clear and well formed but the page as a whole looks untidy or boring. Your handwriting should be much improved by now. It should be legible and have a uniformity that is pleasing to the eye.

Look at the letter, envelope, postcard, or birthday card, cheque and form you wrote at the start of this chapter (*see* page 12).

First look at the letter, since this is probably the most revealing.

You will need a pencil, ruler and tracing paper or thin typing paper.

Put the tracing paper over your letter and block in all the lines of writing and the outside edges of the paper. This way you can see the pattern of your writing on the page. Do you like the look of it? Have you ever considered doing it any other way? (It is interesting that a member of one class said that if she had been

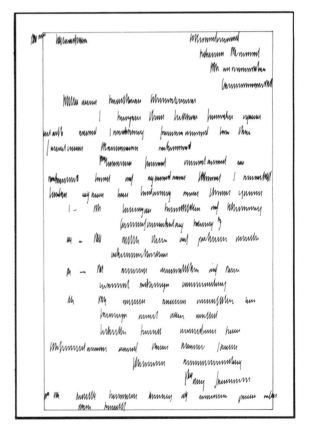

typing the letter, the arrangement would have been more organised and she had never considered applying such thought to a handwritten letter.)

On the same piece of tracing paper, draw the margins you have used around your block of writing. Do you consciously use margins, not only on the left-hand side but, also, top and bottom and on the right side which, obviously, cannot be regular? The white edges of the paper should act as a frame for your written area. The width of the frame depends upon the size of paper and, ideally, should be in a ratio of one on each side and at the top, to one-and-a-half at the bottom. Do some experiments to decide what you prefer.

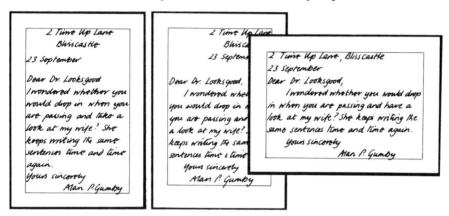

Margins of a letter may be of several different proportions.

Still on the same piece of tracing paper, draw vertical lines wherever there is a new inset, such as for photographs, the lines of the address, the date and the signing off point.

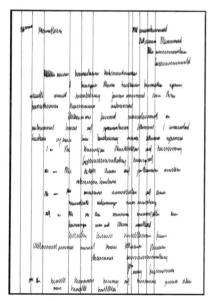

Treauban,
PLENTYWOOD
Montana,
MA 10036.

6th December 1984

Dear Julie,

    I hope you are feeling well, I am fine. I hope you have settled in at College by now and have made many new friends. How is the course? Not too m... ious lessons to put up with.

    Do you see much of your brothers It is a huge place so I suppose you ra I hope the rest of your family is fine a Hope to see you before Christmas, w

---

Bath Cottage
Woolley
Bude

8th December

...forward to seeing you at Christmas. ...esterday, the 7th, that I heard you ... be joining us, since Bay and Jan ...y for Christmas ...know, mum's parents are also coming ..., so it'll be the first time, in years, ... have seen them

---

Lane End, Leighton Buzzard

January 23rd.

Dear Margaret,

... for your letter. So glad you are feel- ...and will be able to come for the week ...us hope for fine weather so that we can

---

15th March '85

Cleave farm,
St. Gennys,
Bude,
Cornwall,
EX230BR

Dear Catherine,

    I hope you are well. Thanks for your letter. It sounds as though you had a lovely holiday.

    Yesterday I went shopping in Plymouth and got some lovely new clothes. In the evening we went to the Barbican theatre and saw a very good performance of Hamlet which I really enjoyed.

    When do you break up for your Easter holidays? I hope you are still coming down to stay with us. Are you?

    I hope your Mum has fully recovered from her operation and is feeling mu...

Heronsmead,
Avening,
Near Tetbury,
Gloucestershire.
January. 7th.

... Doris,

...e just returned from a walk in Minster ...wish you could have been with me as I ... much you would have enjoyed it. ...oods are mainly beech and oak, and ...ay downhill from Minster church to the ... below where the Valency River rushes ...bles over rocks and boulders in its path ...ay to the sea. The fallen leaves made a ...my carpet underfoot, and here and there ...usters of holly berries made glowing ... ...ile a small ...o encouragement.

Hantergantick, St Breward, Bodmin.   1.1.85

Dear Mrs Moore,

I am so sorry that my husband and I will be unable to attend the Coffee Evening on January 4th which

---

This page shows several different ways of laying out the address on a letter.

The result of this may surprise you, especially if you had to draw eight or more vertical lines. Seen as a block pattern you may realise your page looks untidy or confusing. Do you need so many insets? A long address and the date could account for the majority, so it is worth spending some time experimenting with other formats.

Using tracing paper, block in different arrangements until you find one you like. Then try it in writing.

Next, consider the insets for new paragraphs and the conclusion of your letter. Could these be simplified?

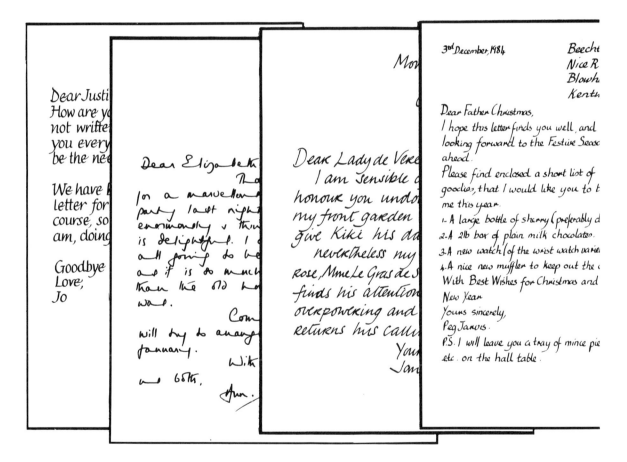

You should have fewer problems with the horizontal layout. The space between the lines of writing should be clear, but you may need to consider leaving larger gaps between the address and the main content of your letter, or between paragraphs. Short letters should not be crammed into the top part of the paper. Conventional writing paper comes in various sizes and you should buy a size

This example shows different ways of setting out the paragraphs in a letter.

33

Waxwell Farm House, Bencubbin, Launceston.
7·XII·84

Dear Brigid,
Thank you for your invitation to visit you and your family next week-end, I would be delighted.

On Friday I shall travel by Fry's Coach to Plymouth and another coach from there to Weymouth. I should be with you at approximately 4·30 pm.

I look forward to seeing you all.

much love
Marie.

356, Sioux Avenue,
Richmond,
Virginia,
U.S.A. 23226.
9ᵗ December, 1984.

My dear Kaye,
Thank you so much for my birthday present — it was good of you to remember the day! And it was good of you to choose a Dylan Thomas I haven't read.
Incidentally we studied Dylan Thomas at Biddy's literature class last year, but it was mostly his poetry and very little of his prose. This book looks to be a good mixture of both.
Again, thank you for your thought.

Love,
Muriel.

Peel's Cottage,
Windham,
Kendal.
3rd December.   Cumberland. MA34 OBE.

Dear John,
        Having returned safely to the sticks I felt I must put pen to paper to say what a pleasure it was to see you again after so many years. Your choice of Restaurant was as always superb. I am not sure we shall be able to compete when you come down in May.
    I have contacted Bill and Peter and they both will be able to come down during your stay.
    Yours as ever
        Geoffrey.

Trevean
Trevenning
St Tudy

3 December.

Dear Fiona,
        Thank you for ringing me last night. I shall arrive at Paddington on Sunday.
        Could you please ask the boys what they would like for Christmas and let me know.
        I am so looking forward to seeing you.

        Love from
        Mary.

This shows the improved handwriting and layout of the letters shown on page 8.

10 x	Heidi Anne	35	00
15 x	Caroline	40	00
20 x	Lady Isobel Barnet	70	00
10 x	Mʳˢ Lovel Sᵗ		
30 x	Stan Cash		
20 x	Cloverdale		
30 x	Floral City		

70	Christmas cards	7	00
15	Christmas wrapping paper		75
10	Red candles	2	00
4	Golden table decorations	2	40
1	Christmas tree	3	10
20	Table napkins		72

BARCLAYS BANK PL
30A MARKET PLACE, CAMELFOR
CORNWALL, PL32 9PD

Pay John Brown

Ten Pounds only

Cheque No.   Branch No.   Account No.

⑂700611⑂ 20⑃17591: 2804

BARCLAYS BANK PLC
30A MARKET PLACE, CAMELFORD,
CORNWALL, PL32 9PD

December 8ᵗʰ 1984

20-17-59

Pay Higgins and Sprogg   or order

one hundred pounds   £100

Cheque No.   Branch No.

⑂700611⑂ 20⑃175

Dear Linda and Suzy

We are going to Plymouth
on the Fry's bus to do
some Christmas
...

Linda and Suzy
2 Stone Flats
...

Came here for the day — the
view is superb. I'm sure Alan
would love to paint it – church,
sea, harbour, and what a
coastline! It's breathtaking
coming down the hill towards
Boscastle itself ~ you have
to be strong-minded to
keep your eyes on the road.
    Love to you both, M.

Deli
Delabole
North Cornwall

26:ii:85

After Launceston, turn right
... min Moor. When you
... A39, turn Left,
... following the signs
...

Mʳˢ. Alan Houlden,
2, College Avenue,
GRANTLEY.
GR1. 1RS.

    Philippa

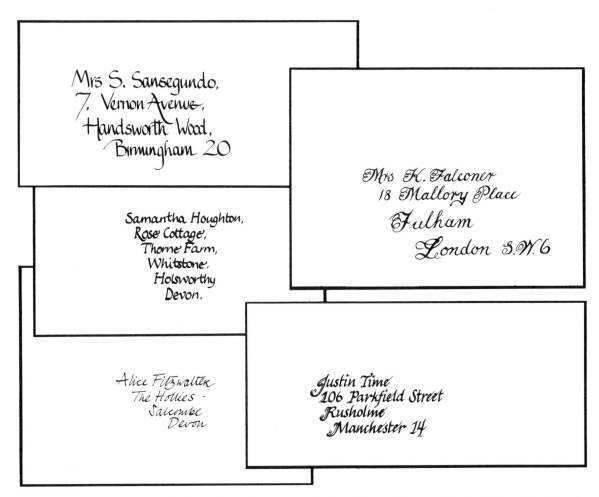

Mrs S. Sansegundo,
7, Vernon Avenue,
Handsworth Wood,
Birmingham 20

Samantha Houghton,
Rose Cottage,
Thorne Farm,
Whitstone,
Holsworthy
Devon.

Mrs K. Falconer
18 Mallory Place
Fulham
London S.W. 6

Alice Fitzwalter
The Hollies
Salcombe
Devon

Justin Time
106 Parkfield Street
Rusholme
Manchester 14

and shape that suits your style of writing and layout. It should be related to the average number of words you write per line.

Look at your letter. What is the average number of words on each line? If it is under five, you should use a larger piece of paper, and if it is over eleven, your paper should be smaller or the margins slightly larger.

Now, it is time to practise. It may help to rule in pencil the vertical lines for the margins, address and paragraph insets until your new layout becomes familiar.

Rewrite the letter you wrote at the beginning. Does it look better? A good handwritten letter should be a pleasure to write and to receive. Sadly, with typewriters and the telephone, fewer people write letters today but, even so, the first impression you make is often by letter. Many employers or college principals prefer applications to be handwritten, feeling that much of your personality is revealed thereby.

Your choice of envelope is also important. The size should be related to the size of the paper and allow for easy folding. The shape, squarish or long and thin, is a matter of preference.

Look at the envelope you addressed at the beginning. Does it appeal to the eye, and could the postman read it? If not, experiment with different layouts to find one you like. Ideally, the address should start just above half way down or at half way to allow for the Post Office stamp and be placed centrally or a little to the left of centre. The length of the address and the size of your writing will determine the actual position.

The methods you have used to analyse your letter writing can be applied to other pieces of handwriting.

Rewrite the card, the cheque and the form and compare them with those you did at the beginning.

There should be a considerable improvement in legibility and style with a growing consciousness of the design of your writing on a page. Further improvement is a matter of constant practice and a continuing pride in the way you present yourself in writing. You may be encouraged now to develop your handwriting skill to produce more formal writing and lettering, which you can use to design your own greetings cards, posters, menus or brochures, or even simply for the pleasure of producing a page of beautiful writing.

ABCDEFGHIJKLM

abcdefghij

ace imn ors uvw xyz

ABCDEF GHIJKL MN OP QRSTU VWX YZ

Part Two

Lettering and Layout

Materials, equipment and working area for the
designer at home.

Part Two

Lettering and Layout

The shapes of letters are beautiful in themselves. In formal writing they take on an individuality which means that they must be executed with flow and precision. The work you did in the first chapter will have helped considerably in developing the uniformity of your style so you will find it easier to form well-shaped, consistent letters. It is for you to decide whether or not to adopt a traditional style, such as italic writing, but this could take a long time to do fluently, particularly if there are many quirks in your handwriting which need to be ironed out. If there is a relationship between your informal writing and your lettering style, there will be a continuation of your natural rhythm in writing. The first stages of achieving this will be slow and need much practice.

Basic Materials
and Equipment
You will need:

- Plenty of paper. Standard ruled file paper will give you guide lines, or use thin typing paper, detail paper or bond paper over a guide sheet ruled with lines about 5 mm ($\frac{1}{4}$ in) apart.
- Two soft pencils (2B) and a harder pencil (H or HB).
- Ruler, scissors.
- Your ordinary fountain pen.
- Italic pen lettering set including nibs fine, medium and broad and B2, B3, B4, plus any other writing tools you may have: a carpenter's pencil, conté crayon, felt-tip pens with chisel shaped tips, a square brush, a round brush, round-hand pen (or dip-pen) with italic nibs or script nibs, poster pens with broader nibs.
- Ink: Black, non-waterproof.

Make sure you are well-organised, have the desk top raised to a reasonable slope and that you are sitting comfortably. The paper should be square to your body. Left-handers will need to adapt to this writing position for large-scale lettering.

Writing Patterns

First of all, be realistic and see what you have to deal with.

Use your ordinary pen or a pencil to write two or three lines in upper and lower case twice or three times the size you normally write. Then, write out the alphabet in lower case (small letters) and again in capitals.

This will reveal many problems such as loss of rhythm, inconsistency of slope, wobbly lines and badly formed letters. The small letters in italic and copperplate may vary in detail but basically the shapes and proportions of the letters are the same. Some of the capital letters are different in formation in the two styles. A simple form of both italic and copperplate letters is demonstrated on the next two pages. When practising, only use the letters which relate to your own style. The movements for certain letters are similar and these are grouped together to make practice easier. Related writing patterns will help you to get the rhythm.

Write on every fourth line so that your writing will be much larger than is normal. Work with a pencil or a pen that you can use easily. Practise these writing patterns and the small letters that relate to your writing until you can do them well.

**Formation of
Letters**

When you feel you have practised these enough, rewrite the alphabet in small

Italic-based handwriting patterns, (left).

Copperplate handwriting patterns, (right).

letters and compare it with the one you did at the beginning. You may realise that some of your letters previously had been carelessly formed. On the whole an oval-shaped letter is more elegant than a circular letter. Keeping stems parallel is difficult enough on a large scale but can you keep all up and down strokes parallel in letters such as h, m, n, u and y? The little upstrokes of the joins should have a sharp curve which would touch or join the next letter about half way up or slightly higher. This produces an upturned 'V' shape which is important for the look of your writing. The 'V' shape should be apparent also, where a curve goes into or out from a stem. Loops, if you use them, should always be slender.

Joining the small letters will come as a natural result of the extension of the curved upstroke at the end of each letter. Some letters do not join logically and should be left separate. A few join with a horizontal stroke.

Write a few words to see if you know instinctively where to join and which kind of join you use. Then check with the examples on the top of page 44.

An oval-shaped letter is more elegant than a circular letter. (Line 1).

Try to keep all stems and joining strokes parallel. (Line 2).

The upstrokes of joins should have a sharp curve. (Line 3).

The upturned 'V' shape is important in joins. (Line 4).

Where a curve goes into or out from a stem the 'V' shape should be apparent. (Line 5).

Loops should be slender and not overlap. (Line 6).

The capital letters are more difficult to do well on a large scale as most of the letters have long straight stems which tend to wobble or go off course!

Both italic and copperplate capitals are illustrated but only work from the style that relates to your writing. Copy the letters first to make sure that you do the strokes in the right order. This will matter later when you use a broad pen.

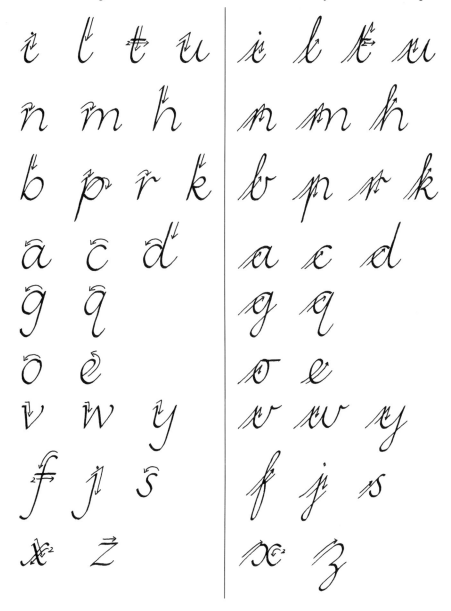

Small letters in a simple italic, (*left*).

Small letters in a simplified copperplate, (*right*).

Joins common to italic and copperplate. (*Top three lines*).

Horizontal joins in italic. (*Line 4*).

Horizontal joins in copperplate. (*Line 5*).

Looped joins in copperplate. (*Line 6*).

Then trace them a few times to get the rhythm, and after that practise them until you can do them well.

Simplified italic capital letters.

Now rewrite the alphabet in capitals and compare it with your first attempt. Capital letters seem to be less personal which is probably why they are used by anonymous letter writers! Is it possible to relate those you have just done to your normal handwriting capitals? It may take time for your large-scale, formal writing and lettering to become personally identified.

Continue writing on a large scale with pencil or your ordinary pen and write several consecutive lines using capitals and small letters. This could be a description, a poem or a recipe.

**Experiments with
Writing Tools**
When you were practising your handwriting, one of the considerations was the

ABCDEFGHIJ
KLMNOPQRS
TUVWXYZ 12345678
abcdefghijklmnopqrstuvw

add bananas and milk
of a dream, remembered
One measure brandy
Compliments and

pen you used. You will have realised that the right pen could transform your writing and improve your style. So it is with lettering. You will not be satisfied to continue working with a pencil or a fine pen. The next stage is to practise with a range of writing tools suitable for large-scale work. Most of these will have a chisel-shaped nib or tip and you will find that the movements needed to use them are more easily learned on a large scale.

First, experiment with the writing tools you have: a broad nib fountain pen, a round-hand pen (or dip-pen), a felt-tip calligraphy pen, conté crayon, a flat brush, a carpenter's pencil and two pencils tied together. Hexagonal pencils tie together more easily. Shave down the inside edges so that the points will be closer and bind them with masking tape. If you are left-handed, set the pencils with one higher than the other, like a left oblique pen nib, as this will be easier for you to use.

The most difficult thing to control is holding the writing tool in the same position to produce lines and shapes that are consistent in thickness and thinness. Check the way you are holding your pen, the position of the paper and

(*From left to right*) 1. Fountain pen with broad italic nib for right-handers; 2. Fountain pen with left oblique broad italic nib for left-handers; 3. Round-hand pen (or dip pen) with broad nib; 4. Felt-tip calligraphy pen; 5. Conté crayon; 6. Flat brush; 7. Carpenter's pencil; 8. Two pencils bound together for a right-hander; 9. Two pencils bound together for a left-hander.

your sitting position. You must be able to move your arm and hand freely across the page. Left-handers may find it more difficult to adapt. Left oblique nibs are much easier to use but not all writing tools are available with these. Experiment with the position of the paper so that you can work easily.

It is important that the angle of a broad-nib pen to the guide lines remains constant. This will produce thick and thin lines in the same place each time.

Use the writing tool you found the easiest to control. Double pencils or a carpenter's pencil will give you a freer action at this stage.

Practise writing patterns and letters with the angle of the writing tool constant. There are several variations you could try.

Straight or parallel to the guide lines, at 20°, 30°, 45° and 90° to the guide lines.

Which angle do you prefer? Choose one and keep to it for the next few experiments. Holding the writing tool at a constant angle is one problem. Uniformity of the letters and spacing is another.

Guide Sheets

It is the time to produce your own guide sheet and you will need several, depending upon the width of the nib and the size of the letters. This is not as daunting a task as it sounds because if the proportion of your letters remains constant you can produce one sheet and have it reduced or enlarged on a photocopying machine.

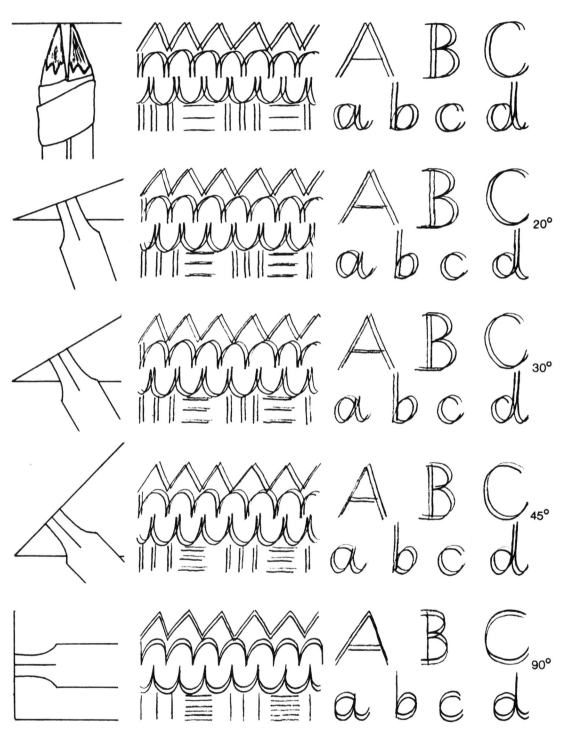

The angle of the broad-nib writing tool to the guide lines should be constant. Several variations are possible: (*From top to bottom*) Straight or parallel; 20°; 30°; 45°; 90°.

First, you must decide on the heights of ascenders and descenders and capitals relative to the height of the small letters or 'x' height. This should be related to the width of the nib and there are several variations.

Measure your own letters to get some idea of what proportion would suit you. Do you prefer bold or elegant letters, short or long ascenders and descenders? Will your capitals be the same height as letters with ascenders or slightly shorter? Experiment with different proportions. How many pen widths will equal the 'x' height? You may find you have to compromise for your choice to be suitable for your hand. When you have decided, rule up your guide sheet as carefully as you can. On a large scale, leave about one pen width between the descender line and the next ascender line. It helps to put the base line as a thicker line. This sheet can be reduced, enlarged, or printed the same size by a photocopier to give you a range of sizes suitable for small and large-scale lettering and for formal handwriting. Vertical margins can be added and you could rule parallel vertical or sloping lines as a guide to the slope of your letters. Do this in pencil to avoid confusion.

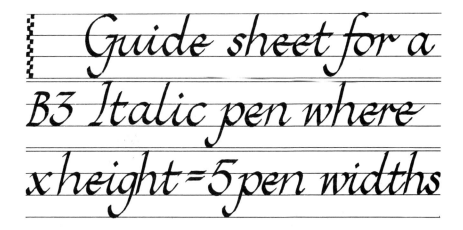

Ruling up the original guide sheet will take you some time. Have it photo-copied and store it safely for future use. (My cat loves sitting on paper!) Stick or

49

tape the guide sheet to a piece of card. If you work with paper of 85 gsm (45 lb) or less you will be able to see the lines of your guide sheet through it. Use sticky tabs to hold your work in position. This system is ideal for practising your lettering, and invaluable later if you make use of photocopying and other forms of printing for reproducing your work.

Practise the letters again and see whether you can make them uniform.

Spacing

The next problem is spacing the letters. When you are using upper and lower case the rules applied to your handwriting will apply here. Leave enough room between letters for the upstrokes or horizontal joins and leave a space of a letter 'o' between words.

Capitals are more difficult. If you use even spacing between all capital letters, as type-setting does, you will sometimes get awkward spaces which divide words. Try writing these words: GROAN, LAWN, SOAP, AVIATE, ACRE.

Could be evenly spaced but see what happens here:

Apparent overlapping will be necessary:

It is better to develop a good eye for what looks right in spacing capital letters in a word. Make a habit of considering two or three together as a pattern in black and white. Look at words in capitals in newspapers, books, advertising material, company names and house names and learn to assess good letter spacing.

Spacing between words when using capitals only can be more flexible. It depends on what is being written, the style and size of the letters. If you are not sure, use a letter 'J' as the minimum and an 'O' as the maximum space between words.

USING CAPITALS ONLY
SPACING BETWEEN WORDS
CAN BE MORE FLEXIBLE

While you are thinking about spacing, you could check the comparative widths of your capital letters. The vertical or sloping lines on your guide sheet will help. Certain letters should be narrow, about half as wide as they are high:
– B, E, F, L, P, S and, possibly, R, Y, K, and, obviously narrower, I and J.

Medium size letters are about three quarters as wide as they are high:

– A, H, N, T, U, V, X, Z and, possibly, R, Y, and K. M and W are as wide or wider than they are high and C, D, G, O and Q are based on a circle. This applies to Roman capitals but you may prefer yours to be proportionately narrower.

Exact proportions are not essential, although this explanation may help if you feel some of your letters look squashed or clumsy.

Try writing a few words in capitals to see if they are improving in shape and uniformity, and that they are well spaced.

MUCH IN LITTLE
SUMMER NIGHTS
BIRMINGHAM BUDE
DOWN THE CLIFF SIDE

Decorative Letters

Many forms of lettering have serifs or flourishes, an added line embellishment at the top and bottom of letters which seems to finish them off and makes them look attractive. Some are produced as a result of lifting the pen and adding a tag, and some by extending the first stroke or end of the letter. So far, the letters you have done have been straight-stemmed and probably made with even pressure on the pen. Holding the pen at a constant angle produces thick and thin lines and varying the pressure emphasises this. Those of you who were taught copperplate writing properly should remember how important it was to change pressure to produce thick and thin lines with a fine flexible pen.

Try these writing patterns, using pressure when doing the wide downstrokes and releasing it on the thin upstrokes.

Pressure should be increased on the downstrokes and released on the upstrokes.

Look at the development of an 'I' and take care that these 'hooks' top and

52

bottom do not allow the stem to develop into an enlongated 'S'. The action is made with a deliberate change of pressure and not by a flick or sudden lifting of the pen. Those of you who find straight stems difficult to do will be pleased to adapt to this more flowing line.

If you combine the vertical and the horizontal strokes the straight letters will have serifs. If you use the small drag strokes at the end of a horizontal line, make sure that it is a fine line.

In a copperplate-based lettering you will tend to develop flourishes rather than serifs. Practise these movements first.

Now try them leading into or extending a letter. Take care that they are not over extended or too thick or you will lose the elegance of this script.

Any embellishment should be done with an easy flow and rhythm. Working on a large scale will help you to develop this. Practise all your letters using serifs or flourishes with double pencils, or a carpenter's pencil, which you will find easier to control. When you have become familiar with the movements, change to using a broad B3 or B4 italic pen or, with a copperplate-based script, you may prefer a finer nib. A pen will produce much sharper letters than pencils. Remember, the nib may need replacing after much use. Better results can be achieved using a round-hand pen (or dip-pen) with italic or script nibs but these are more difficult to use. Use a brush to feed ink into the reservoir as dipping the pen in the ink pot will flood the nib. Expert calligraphers would recommend that you use a round-hand pen (or dip-pen) but you may be happier learning with the italic fountain pen.

Try some of the writing patterns to get the feel of the pen. You will find that upstrokes have to be made by releasing pressure or the pen will scratch on the paper. Most letters will have to be made with several strokes to avoid this.

Using a broad-nibbed pen more strokes are needed to make individual letters. The pen will not go easily 'uphill'.

Copperplate is essentially continuous. Use a nib which is sufficiently soft and flexible to do this.

Lettering Related to Handwriting

It has been our aim to develop a personal style of lettering derived from an improved handwriting. You have studied examples of basic italic or copper-plate letters which will have modified your badly formed letters. Many of you will have a mixture of styles and this is acceptable if you are consistent within your own limitations.

Use the three or four lines you wrote at the beginning of this section as a guide sheet or have a good example of your handwriting greatly enlarged by a photo-copier and work over this. Put a piece of thin paper over the writing, work with the broad pen and try ways of making your writing more formal. The broad pen, a constant angle, serifs or flourishes, a consciousness of the shape of each letter done with an easy rhythm and flow will produce a style of lettering that is recognisable as your own.

This is my LARGE writing
This is my LARGE writing
Nibs VARY in width
Nibs VARY in width

Capitals when enlarged tend to conform to accepted styles. Look at your normal handwriting capitals and compare them with those you have just been doing. Can they be more closely related? The addition of serifs or flourishes will make a difference but if they are to be used with lower case letters based on your handwriting they should relate to them.

**Experiments with
Proportions and
Tools**
All the work so far has been on a large scale. Try using narrower guide lines and a smaller nib size and reduce in two or three stages to your normal handwriting size.

Posters, notices, invitations and so on are likely to need several sizes of writing,

LETTERING *LETTERING* **LETTERING**
large writing *large writing* large writing
Handwriting *Handwriting* Handwriting

lines of capitals only, and upper and lower case letters, all on one piece of paper, so it is important that there is a 'family likeness' in your writing and lettering.

You may need variations on your basic style to suit the occasion. Those can be achieved by changing the writing tool and the size of your letters, so experiment with the tools you have.

- Two pencils tied together worked well, so try two felt-tip pens of different sizes. Felt-tip pens are available in a range of colours and tip shape and size and are useful when notices have to be done quickly.
- Broad and very broad poster pens produce good sharp letters but are more difficult to control.
- Use a broad brush and a fine brush.
- Draw the outside shape of letters and fill in or paint the background to reverse the letters so they are white on black instead of black on white.
- Try using a broad pen, twisting and turning it to exaggerate the thick or thin parts of a letter.
- Use a broad pen or brush to make a simple letter and then use a fine pen or brush for serifs or flourishes. This technique could be developed to produce decorative letters similar to those used in early manuscripts to show where the text started. Try designing your own but remember that the letter must be recognisable.
- A quick way to make large, simple letters is to cut them out from strips of paper.
- Make your own stencils from strong paper or card. You can draw around these or use spray paints. This is a useful method for short notices which have to be repeated.

Experiment with the proportions of your letters. How do they look if tall and thin, or short and fat, or with exaggerated thicks and thins? Try making them conform to a square shape, a rectangle or a circle. (*See* page 38.)

Type Styles
There are hundreds of styles and sizes of lettering in print. Many type-faces

ABCDEFGIHJKLMNOPQ
RSTUVWXYZ
a b c d e f g h i j k l m n o p q r s t u v w x y z

ABCDEFGHIJKLM
NOPQRSTUVWXYZ
abcdefghijklmnopqrstuvwxyz

ABCDEFGHIJKL
MNOPQRSTUVW
XYZ abcdefghijklm
nopqrstuvwxyz

ABCDEFGHIJKLM
NOPQRSTUVW
XYZ abcdefghijklmn YZ
ABCDEFGHIJKLM
NOPQRSTUVWX

Upper and lower case alphabets in Perpetua, Gill Sans, Italic, Copperplate and Old
English.

have been developed over the centuries and new ones have been introduced
and accepted. The majority are based on the Roman alphabet but some are
more closely related to handwriting styles of italic, copperplate, and old
English; many modern type styles are done without serifs. The small selection
illustrated above demonstrates the basic variations and they may give you ideas
to modify your own alphabet.

To complete the work in this section, write out an example of your best handwriting, show how it looks with an italic pen, then how it develops into a formal style using upper and lower case, capitals only, and in an increasing scale of sizes. Finally, add any variations on your basic alphabet that you have developed by changing the writing tool or the proportions of your letters.

It will need much practice for your lettering to become rhythmic and consistent but this will develop with the kind of work suggested in the next section on design.

Here is a sample of my usual handwriting —
a fine Italic nib immediately improves the look of it;
for a bold hand, a BROAD nib is useful.

B2 FOR CAPITALS
and any nib gives scope for a flourish or two

above SUN THE GENTLE, WIND.
below TUI THE JOYOUS, LAKE. *The wind*
blows over the lake and stirs the surface of the water.

Thus visible effects of the invisible

MANIFEST THEMSELVES.

Writing notes I take no care
Now important letters they are a different affair

Special notices need some thought

While posters have LETTERING *of a* LARGER *sort*

This is the handwriting which I use every day
An italic pen-nib changes the style of writing.

THESE ARE COPPERPLATE CAPITALS

Part Three

Design and Practical Projects

Trimming copy with cutting knife, steel ruler and set square
in preparation for mounting or paste-up.

Part Three

Design and Practical Projects

Good design should fulfil its purpose and be pleasing to the eye. In using lettering for design it follows that what is written must be legible. Legibility with a good layout will make your design easily understood and attractive. The work you will do with your lettering may fall into several categories:

- A one-off notice, poster, description, etc.
- A notice, brochure, invitation etc. which has to be produced many times by photocopying or professional printing.
- Something that has to be produced several times but which cannot be reproduced by printing.
- Lettering in conjunction with drawings or using colour which may be a one-off job or for reproduction.

Some of these will need no more materials and equipment than you have already. Others will need new materials and equipment to help you to work more efficiently. Study the list below to assess what you have, and think carefully about those that you have not, before buying something you may never need. First, consider your working situation:

Working Area

You need somewhere in the house which can be set up for your work and this should be well organised. Your table or desk should have a working top raised to 20°–30°. A piece of 20 mm ($\frac{3}{4}$ in) chipboard 900 mm × 600 mm (36 in × 24 in) will be large enough for most purposes. This can be raised by supporting it on a piece of timber. There are sophisticated technical drawing desks on the market which are beautiful but very expensive! Cover your board with a piece of soft card, or blotting paper or a few sheets of paper to give you a resilient working surface. A raised board is better for writing but you will need a flat area on which to keep your writing tools, ink, paper and other equipment. A trolley might well suit this purpose and can be stored out of the way when not in use. A good light is essential and day light is best. Ideally, the light should come from behind your shoulder but often this is not possible. Experiment to find the best place. Choose a chair or stool that is comfortable, supports your back to keep you upright and allows you to put both feet on the floor, or if your work top is higher, use a footstool. My work top is 900 mm (36 in) high so that I can work standing up when necessary but I need a high chair and footstool when sitting.

Materials and Equipment

Writing tools: a fountain pen with a soft, round nib and a range of italic nibs – fine, medium, broad, B2, B3 and B4 (left oblique for left-handers), round-hand pen (or dip-pen) with steel nibs for italic and flexible nibs for copperplate; poster pens with much broader nibs; technical drawing pen; felt-tip calligraphy pens; flat and round brushes; pencils, H or HB for ruling guide lines, 2B for roughing out, two 2B pencils tied together; a carpenter's pencil; conté crayon; ruling pen.

Non-waterproof black ink; waterproof indian ink (harmful to all pens but may be needed for outdoor work. Always wash the pen immediately after use); coloured inks.

Poster paints or gouache or watercolour paints.

● Process white: a water-soluble white paint for touching up work for photographic reproduction.

● Putty rubber.

Good straight ruler 300 mm (12 in) and a longer metal ruler to use for cutting card and paper: a piece of carpet edging works very well.

Set square, compass, dividers.

Glues: aerosol spray glue is invaluable as it allows for repositioning and does not crinkle or stain thin paper. A stronger glue like PVA or cow gum will be needed for thicker paper and card.

Cutting knife: those with snap-off blades are good.

Masking tape and sticky tabs for positioning work.

Scissors.

Blotting paper and tissues or cotton cloth for wiping pens.

● Paper: A4 (210 mm × 297 mm or $8\frac{1}{4}$ in × $11\frac{3}{4}$ in) Bond paper or thin typing paper 45 gsm (25 lb) is useful for practising over a guide sheet and for finished work that will be pasted up for reproduction. A4 85 gsm (45 lbs) paper for better quality and surface; A4 ruled file paper for practising; tracing paper; thick card – Bristol board has a good surface but it is expensive. You should be able to find a suitable card about 750 micron (10 sheet) at your local printers but check that it is not absorbent. A range of coloured papers and card is useful for mounting work. You may need some paper in bigger sizes for large-scale work, a good quality

smooth cartridge paper and a thinner layout paper or detail paper.
- Guide sheets: you should have made yours by now (*see* page 49).
- A dictionary and reference books.
- Light box: not essential but useful for tracing work, producing colour separations for a printer, assembling cut-out work over a guide sheet. It does away with the need for tracing paper and because the light shines through the paper you can use a better quality one for your artwork. Experiment with a piece of glass over a light or put some work against a window to see if you would find this a piece of equipment worth having. Those which you can buy are expensive and it is quite easy to make one.

Basically, you need a box about 600 mm × 450 mm (24 in × 18 in) and 150 mm (6 in) deep. The top is a piece of 4 mm ($\frac{3}{16}$ in) glass or perspex. The glass should be supported by beading fixed to the box just below the top edge. A small strip light fixed to the bottom will shine sufficient light through the glass and two or three pieces of 145 gsm (72 lb) paper.

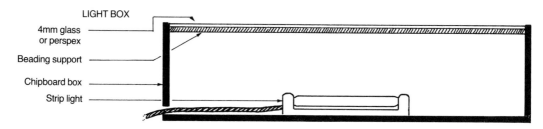

Light box. Made from 4 mm glass or perspex, chipboard box, strip light, and beading to support glass or perspex.

Obviously, not all these materials and equipment are necessary. Much depends upon the work you will do and you can add to your basic range as the need arises. Look after what you have, there is nothing worse than settling down to a job to find pens that need washing or paper that is creased.

You should be ready now to try out different ways of using your lettering. We will consider layout, preparing work for printing, other methods of reproducing work, and lettering with drawings and using colour.

Layout
Work on thin paper over your guide sheet using a pencil or double pencils for the larger letters. Make a draft layout for each of four assignments:

A poem or copy for a brochure
An invitation
A poster
A large, short notice

Several points need to be considered:

- The overall size of your paper and the size of the letters should be right for the job. Think about who is going to read it and at what distance.
- The area of writing should be related to the size and shape of the paper. Are the margins reasonable, too small or over generous?
- Do you want a symmetrical or an asymmetrical balance of the writing to the paper?
- Symmetry is easy to assess but not always easy to attain when lettering by hand. To centralise lines of writing on a poster means double the work as you must know accurately the centre point of each line of writing. It is easier when the work is to be printed and this is dealt with later. A block of writing can be symmetrical on the page if you use vertical lines on your guide sheet to give equal margins on both sides. Careful trimming when you have finished is an easy way to achieve a symmetrical page.

Mr & Mrs Christopher Deacon request the pleasure of your company at a Garden Party in aid of the N.S.P.C.C. at 2·0 pm., Saturday, 12th August, 1985 R.S.V.P. Heworth Green, York.	COME TO MARK'S PARTY! Saturday 30th March 2·30 - 6·0 in the Queen's Temple, Stowe R.S.V.P. 4, Home Park

There are no rules for the right balance in an asymmetrical layout but most of us know when it is wrong! Asymmetry can be used to emphasise important sections of the text and is often used when writing is combined with a drawing or design.

Check the vertical divisions on your work as you did when setting out a letter. Too many will be confusing and untidy whereas none at all may be boring. Indenting some lines for paragraphs, or information such as dates or times in a poster, or an address or an invitation, is an effective way of achieving emphasis and only requires an extra vertical line on your guide sheet.

🍷 *THE MANZANILLA CLUB*

Request the pleasure of your company at

A Sherry Tasting Evening

To be held at
The first vinyard on the left.
Bodega Al Fondo

Friday 12ᵗʰ July 1985.
At Sundown
Dress: Flamboyant
R. S. V. P.

Mr and Mrs C.A.N. Doit

Cordially invite : Mr and Mrs B.A. Creep

To the Graduation Party

For their daughter, Achira

To be held at The Leats

Saturday 21ˢᵗ July, 1985 at 8pm.

Dress: Evening   R.S.V.P.

Next, consider horizontal spacing in the lines of writing. Are they clearly separated? Should there be a larger gap between one part and another to make it more important, or should there be a change in the size of the writing to make the same point?

Midsummer Fair
at Abels Manor
on Sat June 21ˢᵗ '85
Period Dress
All are Welcome

Midsummer Fair
at Abels Manor
on Sat June 21ˢᵗ '85
Period Dress
All are Welcome

Now, look at the words. Is the scale right for the job? Too few words per line can lead to a ragged right-hand margin or irritating breaks in words to avoid this. Too many words on a line make reading difficult. Is the spacing between words right? When using upper and lower case together, remember the space should be the width of one letter 'o' and, using capitals only, no less than the letter 'J'. However, if you want a neat right-hand margin, the allowance must be made between words and not between the letters of a word.

JUMBLE SALE
DAVIDSTOW HALL
on 23rd January

Finally, look at the individual letters. Is the slope parallel? If not, use a guide sheet with parallel vertical or slightly sloping lines to help you. Are the letters well-formed and is the space right between each letter in the word?

Now, consider each of your draft layouts in turn and make the necessary adjustments.

It may not be practical for your assignment to be produced on paper thin enough to work over a guide sheet. If you have a light-box you can use thicker paper over your rough draft and lightly pencil in the guide lines and wording. Working on card your guide lines will have to be measured and drawn. Feint lines should be drawn with a sharp H or HB pencil. If it will make you more confident, pencil in the words and then check the width of the pen nib in relation to the height of your letters.

Practise your letters several times on rough paper to get the rhythm of your writing, then take a deep breath, relax and do your lettering!

Trimming and Mounting

Your final copy may need trimming to size and it may look better for mounting on card. Cutting is better done with a knife than with scissors. Use a sharp knife against a steel ruler with your work on card and not a wooden surface as this will blunt the knife. Check your measurements using a set square if necessary. Keep the knife low when cutting and use steady pressure along the line.

FUN WITH PAINT IN PLAYGROUP A WORKSHOP MON. FEB. 4th

AT 8pm AT

BERRIES AVENUE PLAYGROUP

Return to School

All of a sudden
You change again,
Affected by your environment,
becoming hostile,
Defensive,
Afraid,
And with this new front
Believe you are different.
But you can't hide,
Not anywhere.

Jessica Cork.

Trevarrian is a small quiet village only half a mile from Mawgan Porth beach and five miles from Newquay.
There are many attractions for the visitor to this holiday town. Newquay is famous for its five surfing beaches, there is a golf course, tennis courts, bowls, swimming pool, boating lake in Trenance gardens and a zoo nearby. However, if you feel you want to get away from it all, there are magnificent cliff walks.

'YOU'
are invited to an
18th
Birthday Party
on the 16th May
at Bath Cottage
Woolly
Morwenstow

ELIZABETH

THIS IS TO CERTIFY THAT

Geoffrey Quayle

HAS SUCCESSFULLY COMPLETED
AN INTRODUCTORY DIVING COURSE
HELD BY
BUDEHAVEN SUB-AQUA CLUB

DIVING OFFICER *Jacqueline Allan.*

DATE APRIL 7th 1985

INSIDE MY HEAD

Inside my head
    there is a brain.
Inside my brain
    there is a thought,
Inside my thought
    there is an invention,
Inside my invention
    there is a plan,
Inside my plan
    there is a wonder,
Inside my wonder
    there is Me,
  Me,
Inside my head.

Brett Maton.

*Geoffrey and Renée Bayfield
Request the pleasure of
Quentin Crisp's
Company at Dinner on
Thursday 20th October
at 7.30 p.m. for 8 p.m.*

R.S.V.P.

St Morwenna,
Trethevy,
Tintagel.

NORTH CORNWALL

*This is a strange Celtic Country but no longer
forbidding. The sense of the past is strong
Churches like sentinels along the coast, stone
cottages with slate roofs, stone walls edging
fields and roads, old quarries and mines
stone circles and hill forts.*

BEACH PATROL

Mounting your work on card will give added support and a good finish. Choose a suitable colour, place your writing on it and decide the width of your margins, as below:

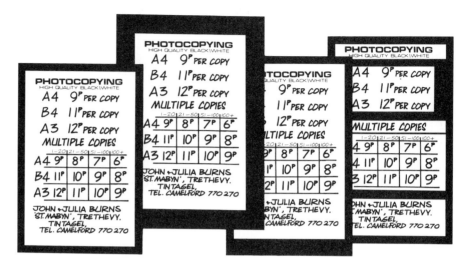

From left to right:

1   Narrow margins with an even ratio $1 - 1 - 1 - 1$.
2   Wide margins with an even ratio.
3   Even margins on the sides and top and a larger space at the bottom.
4   Dividing each line of writing for greater emphasis, or useful if you make a mistake on one line and do not want to rewrite all of it! This can be a means of centralising all your lines of writing.

Use a suitable glue to paste your work in position. Spray glue is the best as long as your paper is not too thick. Cover with scrap paper to press down as your hands may be damp or sticky!

Preparing Work for Printing

Some of the work you do will need to be produced in quantity: posters, invitations, brochures, Christmas cards and so on. In the past, this had to be done by hand or a decision made to use a professional printer. Developments in the quality of photocopying have added a new dimension to the work of the amateur calligrapher and designer. Your original work in black and white can be reduced or enlarged, or printed the same size and copied a hundred times on paper or thin card, for a quarter of the price it would be if done by a professional printer. However, for quality reproduction on thicker card, considerable reductions in size, work in colour and for quantities over five hundred you will get a better and probably cheaper job from the professional.

The way in which you present your work for printing is most important but first you need to understand the possibilities and limitations of the machine you will use.

Most photocopying machines will produce prints at these sizes:

A3   297 mm × 420 mm   ($11\frac{3}{4}$ in × $16\frac{1}{2}$ in)
A4   210 mm × 297 mm   ($8\frac{1}{4}$ in × $11\frac{3}{4}$ in)
B4   255 mm × 360 mm   (10in   × 14in)

Your original work can be reproduced the same size within these limitations. If your original is much smaller you may be able to get two for the price of one copy.

1   Your original half A4 size (A5).
2   Take one print same size.
3   Stick this print next to your original on the same A4 sheet.

Print your copies at A4 same size for double quantity. If the rate for A3 printing is less than double an A4 sheet, the same method could be used for A4 when large numbers of copies are needed.

Much of your work may be improved by having it reduced in size. Work produced at A3 can be reduced to A4 or B4 and, using the same process, work at A4 can be reduced to A5 or B5.

1 Your A3 original can be reduced by about a third to –
2 A4 or –
3 By about a sixth to B4.

When reducing an A4 original to A5, to double the quantity produced, present the A4 original on half of an A3 sheet. Take one copy actual size on A4 and stick this on the other half of the A3 sheet. Ask for an A3 to A4 reduction and this will produce double the quantity of A5 copies on A4 sheets.

Copying from a copy is not always successful. It depends on the quality of the machine and how well it is maintained. Check the darkness or lightness of your copy and, also, that the glass of the machine is clean. If the work is to be printed on both sides of a single sheet, see that the reverse side is printed the same way up! A double-sided brochure can be produced this way.

Getting two for the price of one is more complicated but it can be done if you paste up your artwork correctly.

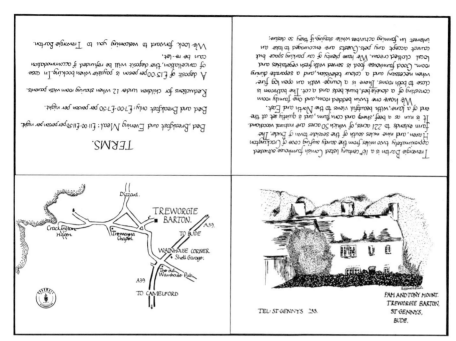

Art work pasted up on A3 sheet. This can be reproduced at the same size or reduced to A4 for a small brochure.

- ● Print the number of copies required.
- ● Leave the original on the machine.
- ● Turn copies over and reverse sides to print.
- ● Cut down the centre lengthways only!

Most machines will also make enlargements.

1. Original A4 copy;
2. First enlargement;
3. Second enlargement from the first enlargement. (Some machines will produce the second enlargement size in one process.)

The increase is not very large and it may be necessary to take a second enlargement from an enlargement to get from A4 to A3, and this can mean a loss of quality in print.

No doubt, these processes appear to be complicated or confusing. If you have not used a photocopier before, take a piece of writing on an A4 sheet to your local copyshop and see what happens when your work is reproduced the same size, reduced and enlarged. You do need to understand the possibilities before you prepare your work to be copied.

Paste-up for
Printing
Original artwork at A3 or A4 can be reduced by about a third to A4 or A5. As most of us write better on a larger scale, take the reduction sizes into account when you are preparing your work for printing.

The procedure for layout of your work is similar to that for a one-off job (page 68). All work should be in black and white, although a soft pencil used firmly will print a charcoal-like line on good copiers. Allow a 12 mm ($\frac{1}{2}$ in) margin all round as sometimes extreme edges do not print. One of the benefits of having your work printed is that you can make full use of pasting up and covering mistakes with white paper or touching up with process white. Pasting-up will not show if you use thin paper. You can write out your lines of copy on paper over a guide sheet, cut the lines of writing into strips, measure the centre if you want the work to be centralised and paste down onto a thicker piece of paper or card. Spray glue is ideal in this instance as it allows for repositioning, which is useful if you change your mind or did not get the lines straight. Word mistakes can be pasted over in the same way. Other mistakes or blots can be painted over with process white as long as you are using waterproof ink.

If your work is smaller than the standard sizes, mount it on an A3 or A4 sheet in a position where trimming will be easy. Check that everything is square, properly pasted down and clean before you have your work copied.

Better quality and more versatile printing is available at your local printers. Sizes are more flexible and there is a wide variety of papers, cards and colours to choose from. It is usually cheaper than photocopying for quantities over 500. There are two methods of printing, letterpress and off-set lithography. In letterpress a block, similar to a lino-cut block but photographically acid-etched in metal has to be made from your artwork. This can be expensive for sizes over A4, unless you are having work printed in thousands, but is a good method for letter headings which are likely to be repeated at a later date.

Paste-up for printing showing two different layouts produced by separating the lines of copy and arranging in two ways. Using thin paper the paste-up lines will not show in printing.

More usual today is off-set litho printing where a photographic plate is made from your work. Large areas of colour are more evenly printed this way, generally it is cheaper and certainly more versatile.

Your artwork can be prepared in a similar way to that for photocopying. You can make use of greater reductions or enlargements. Always state this on your copy.

← —————— *Reduce to 101 mm (4 ins)* —————— →

Take into account the most economic use of paper or card. The printer will buy most of his card as SRA2 (450 mm × 640 mm or $17\frac{3}{4}$ in × $25\frac{1}{4}$ in) which allows for four A4 sheets, plus trimming allowance, or in Royal size (520 mm × 640 mm or $20\frac{1}{2}$ in × $25\frac{1}{4}$ in).

**Other Methods of
Producing
Quantity**

Occasionally you may be asked to produce work in quantity for which photo-copying or printing is not practicable or suitable. It could be a large notice, need to be waterproof, or use several colours. Imagine a situation in which you have to write CRAFT FAIR in letters 100 mm (4 in) high at least twenty times for display outdoors for a week. Obviously, your writing must be waterproof and not fade or curl up in the sun. First, write out the words using double pencils on rough paper. If the letter C is as wide as it is high and the others are related to it you will need a board about 900 mm × 200 mm (36 in × 8 in) with both words on the same line, or 450 mm × 300 mm (18 in × 12 in) if FAIR is written underneath CRAFT.

You may be lucky enough to get someone else to prepare these boards for you but, if not, it is part of your job as designer to do this and to know how they will be fixed in place. Something like hardboard will be necessary to stand up to wind and sun, and a long piece would need battens for support. The board will need a couple of coats of paint if your writing is to be done directly on the surface. There are several ways you could do this notice twenty times:

- The quickest way would be using a 20 mm ($\frac{3}{4}$ in) brush with emulsion paint or oil paint. Draw guide lines, sketch out the letters with double pencils and remember to leave reasonable margins. Set the board in a position where you can move your arm easily. Work quickly enough to keep the rhythm and even slope of your letters. If necessary, touch up with a finer brush.

- Another fairly quick method would be to use two waterproof felt pens tied together. One thicker than the other could be effective.

CRAFT FAIR ▶

- You may prefer to use a pen which is not, of course, suitable for use on board. You would have to write on paper which could then be pasted onto the boards. Many posters are done this way and yours should last for a week.

CRAFT FAIR ⟶

You may lack the confidence to work directly with a brush or pen. There are other methods which take a little longer to prepare but are fairly quick to use.

- Stencils are useful when a short notice has to be produced many times. Cover thin card with self-adhesive vinyl, cut out your letters leaving enough surround for support and use spray paint, remembering to lift the letters carefully to avoid smudging. Paper tends to buckle, unprotected card may warp after it has been used a few times, and ordinary paint may creep underneath the stencil.

You could draw around the letters of your stencil and fill in with paint afterwards. This will be slower but offers of help can be accepted. Waterproof felt-tip pens could provide a quicker alternative.

If you have access to screen printing facilities your letters could be cut out of paper for the stencil and then printed on paper to be pasted on the boards afterwards.

CRAFT-FAIR ▶

Sticky-backed letters can be bought but they are very expensive. You could make your own but it is a tedious occupation without help. The result is effective and could be used when small quantities are needed!

Cut the paper into strips the height of your letters. Then cut the strips into squares for the wide letters, three quarter and half squares for the medium and narrow letters, and a narrower strip for an 'I'.

Simple, bold letters can be cut with scissors or a knife three or four at a time. These can be pasted onto the board using a PVA glue or, much quicker, spray glue adhesive. It would be wise to spray the finished board with polyurethane to protect them.

CRAFT FAIR →

It is possible to use the lino printing method for short notices. Remember the letters must be back to front! You could use lino for a large notice but this is extravagant. Your letters could be cut in thick card with a knife, or in hardboard or three-ply wood with a coping saw or a fret saw. Glue them back to front on a board for support. Use an oil based printing ink with a roller to ink up your block and then print. As with screen printing this may be done more easily on paper than board.

 **CRA**

**Lettering with
Drawings and
using Colour**
Lettering and handwriting may, also, be used in conjunction with drawings,

photographs or maps and possibly using colour. Careful planning is needed to relate the writing to the drawing, one can enhance the other or destroy it. Consider some possible situations: Christmas cards, letter headings, labels for home-made wine or preserves, or illustrating text in a book. Is it the lettering or the drawing, photograph or design which is most important? It is worth spending some time on the draft layout to decide how the two will fit together. Should the drawing or design surround the lettering? Is the writing a title for the drawing or are they intermixed, as on a map?

Illustration of a short passage from *The Old Curiosity Shop* showing the intermixing of drawing and writing.

Write out the wording as it needs to be set, if it is the text that is the more important. Overlay a sheet of tracing paper and experiment with the drawing or design. If the drawing or design cannot be changed, do the writing on tracing paper overlaid on the drawing or cut the writing into strips to experiment with its position.

A one-off job is produced in a straightforward way. If the work is to be printed, remember the advice given earlier about sizes and the way to present your work.

You may want to use colour to enhance your work. There is no problem with a one-off job. You are free to use coloured inks, paints, pencils or felt-tip pens as you wish. The problems arise when you want your work produced in quantity. Full colour printing by off-set litho is very expensive and there are several alternatives you could consider.

- Have the work printed in black and white and mount it on coloured paper or card.
- Produce the outline of the drawing and lettering, have it photocopied and add colour by hand afterwards.
- Produce the coloured drawing or design by screen printing or lino-printing and add the lettering by hand.
- Make use of colour photographs. Brochures and greetings cards can be done this way. Produce your black and white lettering for printing, allowing for the area of the photographs. Several photographic firms provide a service for brochure prints. You send a negative, state the size of print and quantity required, and ask for 'stikapic' fixing. This is an adhesive tape on the back of the photographs which enables quick and easy fixing to your cards.

Making use of colour:
(*From left to right*)
1. Printed work mounted on coloured card;
2. Printed work in outline to be filled in later with coloured ink or paint;
3. Writing printed and coloured photograph stuck on afterwards.

Some photocopying services offer separate colour printing but this is not generally available in the provinces. The results are similar to those obtained from a professional printer but with the advantages of photocopying for small numbers. You need to understand the process of colour separation if you want to produce colour work at a reasonable price. If you send full-colour art work on one sheet to a printer your work will be involved in a complicated and expensive process to separate your colours. There is no alternative for a painting or a photograph. However, you can enhance your own work by using one or two extra colours and providing the separations yourself. For example, consider the process of producing a map with the writing and general design in black, rivers and sea in blue, and roads in brown.

- Make an accurate drawing, put in the names of places, roads etc. and with blue and brown pencils, colour in where necessary. This is your master copy.

- Now, each colour has to be produced in black on a separate sheet. You could use tracing paper but a light-box saves much time and allows all the work to be done on good cartridge paper.
- Tape your master copy on the light-box. Make registration marks x in each corner. Overlay a clean sheet and put in the registration marks. Make the black copy on this sheet.
- Overlay the master copy with another clean sheet to make the blue copy but your work must be done in black.
- Repeat the process for the brown copy.

Check the registration marks and use process white to remove any overlapping of colours where it could be confusing. The printer will make three separate plates and print in the colours required.

As for all work to be printed make sure that your copy is supported on card to keep it firm, covered with thin paper to keep it clean and that your instructions are absolutely clear. Remember to give a reduction size, if necessary, colour of ink to be used, quality of paper or card and the quantity required. Check with your printer that he can do the process wanted and get a quotation from him before authorising him to start work. Seeing your work in print will give you much pleasure so do be sure you do everything right to get the best result possible.

**Ideas and
Suggestions for
Using Lettering**

Once it is known that you are interested in lettering you may find quite a number of assignments coming your way; posters for local clubs and societies, notices at special events, certificates for sports, an inscription for a presentation gift and so on. It is nice to be asked but it may be some time before you feel your lettering is good enough to accept a commission. In the meantime there are many ways in which you can use and develop your skills by writing for your own purposes or to give pleasure to others.

Right from the start you could make a resolution to send letters or cards which are well written. Use a good pen and good paper, sit down at your desk instead of the arm chair, think about the way in which you set out your letter and before long this will become a good habit.

Resolve to fill in order forms and write cheques with a fountain pen. We may encourage the banks to provide blotting paper at their counters again!

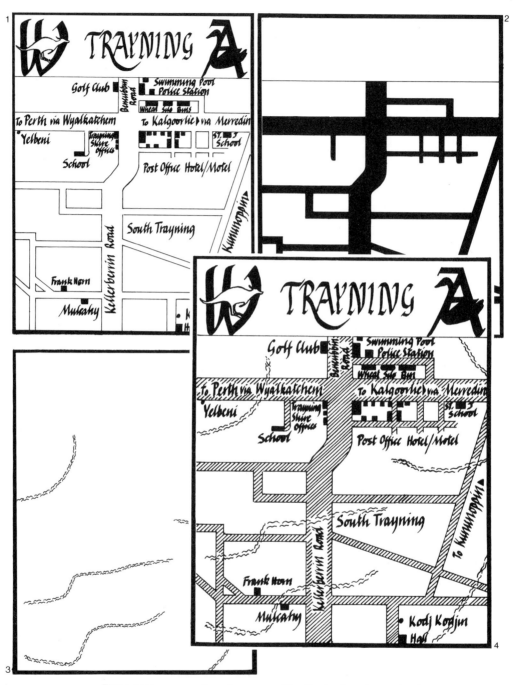

■	Black
▨	Brown
≋	Blue

Three colour separations for a map. The illustration shows the three separate copies needed to print the map in black, brown and blue.

1. (*Top left*) Outline and lettering to be printed in black.
2. (*Top right*) Roads to be printed in brown.
3. (*Bottom left*) Creeks to be printed in blue.
4. (*Bottom right*) Completed copy. (Lettering in black, hatched area in brown, and small wavy lines in blue.) All artwork is produced at the same size in black.

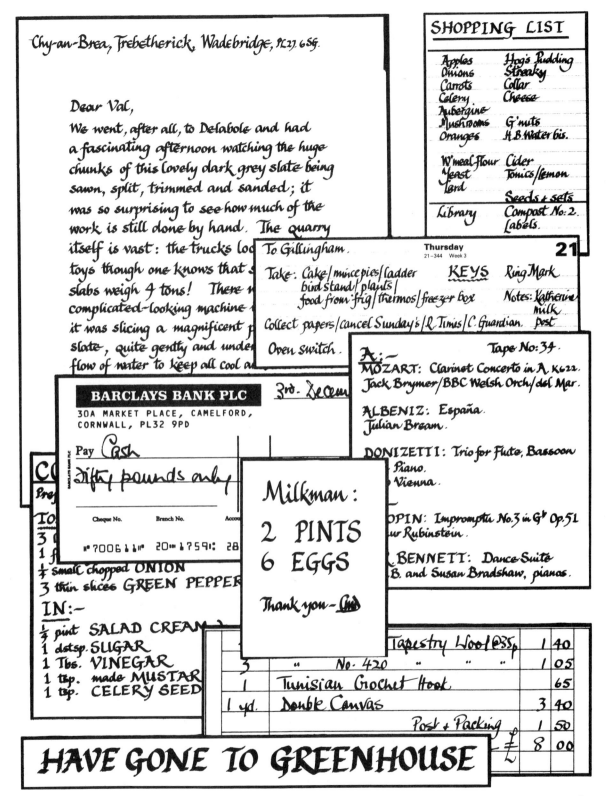

Chy-an-Brea, Trebetherick, Wadebridge, PL27 6SG.

Dear Val,

We went, after all, to Delabole and had a fascinating afternoon watching the huge chunks of this lovely dark grey slate being sawn, split, trimmed and sanded; it was so surprising to see how much of the work is still done by hand. The quarry itself is vast: the trucks loo[k] toys though one knows that s[ome] slabs weigh 4 tons! There [...] complicated-looking machine [...] it was slicing a magnificent p[...] slate, quite gently and unde[r a] flow of water to keep all cool a[...]

SHOPPING LIST

Apples	Hog's Pudding
Onions	Streaky
Carrots	Collar
Celery	Cheese
Aubergine	
Mushrooms	G'nuts
Oranges	H.B. Water bis.
W'meal Flour	Cider
Yeast	Tonics/Lemon
Lard	
	Seeds + sets
Library	Compost No: 2. Labels.

Thursday 21–344 Week 3 — **21**

To Gillingham.
Take: Cake/mince pies/ladder bird stand/plants food from frig/thermos/freezer box
KEYS Ring Mark
Notes: Katherine milk post
Collect papers/cancel Sunday's/R. Times/C. Guardian.
Oven switch.

A:— Tape No: 34.
MOZART: Clarinet Concerto in A. K.622. Jack Brymer/BBC Welsh Orch/del Mar.

ALBENIZ: España. Julian Bream.

DONIZETTI: Trio for Flute, Bassoon [and] Piano. [...] Vienna.

[CHO]PIN: Impromptu No.3 in G♭ Op.51 [Arth]ur Rubinstein.

[...] BENNETT: Dance Suite [...] B. and Susan Bradshaw, pianos.

BARCLAYS BANK PLC
30A MARKET PLACE, CAMELFORD, CORNWALL, PL32 9PD

3rd Dece[mber]
Pay Cash
Fifty pounds only

Cheque No.   Branch No.   Accou[nt]
⑈700611⑈ 20⑈1759⑈ 28[...]

Milkman:
2 PINTS
6 EGGS
Thank you — [initials]

CO[...]
Prep[...]
IO[...]
3 [...]
1 f[...]
¼ small chopped ONION
3 thin slices GREEN PEPPER
IN:—
⅓ pint SALAD CREAM
1 dstsp. SUGAR
1 Tbs. VINEGAR
1 tsp. made MUSTAR[D]
1 tsp. CELERY SEED

		Tapestry Wool @35p	1	40
3	" No. 420 " "		1	05
1	Tunisian Crochet Hook			65
1 yd.	Double Canvas		3	40
		Post + Packing £	1	50
		£	8	00

HAVE GONE TO GREENHOUSE

Instead of writing shopping lists, etc. on the back of old envelopes, use a small tear-off note pad and, if using a pen seems pedantic, use a pencil rather than a biro.

How do you write your daily requests to the milkman, baker or other regular callers? You could produce decent notices in waterproof ink on card and cover with clear plastic film or write them with paint or waterproof felt-tip pen on a board.

Are your telephone and your address book clearly written and well set out? Maybe it is time they were redone!

Do you keep a diary? The problem with many that you buy is that the space allowed for each day is either too small or too large, or the line spacing is wrong for your writing. Buy a book that is right for you and in which you can write as much or as little as you want each day.

Many of us have a household filing system. Is yours properly labelled and easy to refer to? In becoming conscious of your writing quite a number of things will be better organised and save you time in the future. If you are a student, an improved layout and writing in your exercise books or files will benefit you and your tutors.

These suggestions affect the writing that you do every day. As your hand-writing becomes more uniform and rhythmical you will find that formal writing and lettering will be less of an effort to do well and you can enjoy more adventurous lettering and design projects.

Those of you who draw and paint can use drawings and decorative designs with your lettering. If you lack confidence in drawing, you could experiment with ways of decorating your letters using the writing strokes, serifs and flourishes with which you are familiar. Also, you could copy or trace decorative designs which were used for something else, such as oriental carpets or decorative stone and wood carving. Translating these into writing patterns and designs would make them your own. Using writing and decoration around a photograph is another possibility.

Here are some ideas for using formal handwriting and lettering. The practical problems of layout, ways of producing your work, including printing, have been discussed and you may need to refer back to them when developing these projects.

Recipe Book

A recipe book or file could be as straightforward in layout as your telephone or address book. You could make yours more exciting by using your own drawings or photographs properly mounted. Your own special recipes could be photocopied to give to friends. Our local playgroup sold theirs at a food-tasting fund-raising event.

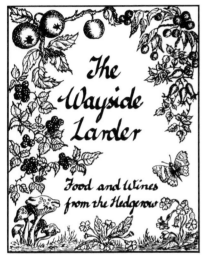

Elderflower Champagne

1 gallon of water   1-1¼ lbs gran. sugar
2 lemons   7 heads of elderflower
2 tablespoons of white wine vinegar

Bring the water to the boil. Add the sugar and stir until dissolved. Allow to get cold. Add the flowers, cut-up lemon and vinegar. Leave for 24 hours, stirring occasionally. Squeeze out the lemon pieces. Strain the liquid into bottles and cork. Chill in the refrigerator before serving. Can be used immediately, but will keep for a year.

Menus

Still thinking of food, you could design menus for special occasions. Many hoteliers lavish money on folders and then fill them with badly written or faintly-typed menus. They would look better and be easier to read in dim lighting if they were well written in black ink and then photocopied. You could offer this service locally.

BAR MENU

Ploughmans Lunch   1 50
Farmhouse Paté   1 86

Sausage & Chips   1 45
Scampi & Chips   2 00
Chicken & Chips   1 75

Sandwiches
        brown or white
        toasted 10p extra
Ham   .95
Cheese   .75
Cheese & Tomato   .80

CANADIAN SUPPER
✽
Fiddlehead Soup

Prairie Chicken with Wild Rice
Asparagus with Hollandaise Sauce
Watercress and Mushroom Salad

Maple Syrup Backwoods Pie
Ice Cream

Cheese

Bottle and Jar
Labels

Do you make your own wine or preserves? You could produce your own 'house label'. You will need to work out a design that generally will suit all, leaving a space for the particular details to be written in later. Your labels can be photocopied, cut to size and fixed to the bottles or jars using spray-glue adhesive.

Labels for Display

Good labelling can be used, also, in a stamp collection, photograph album, work folders and for displays and exhibitions. If you are using sticky-back labels, work out a system of ruling guide lines. In the long run, it saves time and allows you to write more quickly. Labels for display may need mounting on card.

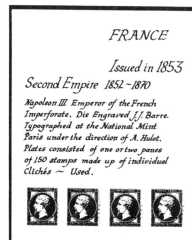 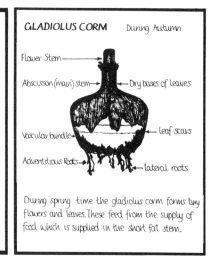

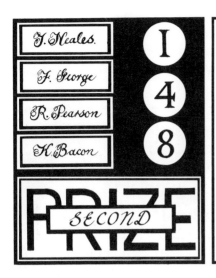

A mahogany fire screen
with Elizabethan sampler

Multiplication
     is vexation
Division is as bad
The rule of three
      doth puzzle me
And practise
      drives me mad

J. Neales.
J. George
R. Pearson
K. Bacon

1
4
8

PRIZE

SECOND

Book Plates

Book plates used to be very popular and still are a good idea if you lend your books to friends. You could design one which includes your name and address, have it photocopied and use spray glue for fixing.

St. Petroc's Church
Trevalga

Butterwell
Davidstow
Camelford

Christmas Cards

The annual problem of Christmas cards can be solved by designing your own. Thinking of a good design is not easy. All the sentimental and well-worn clichés of Christmas come to mind and finding an original way to use them needs inspiration. You could base your design on something personal such as your house, part of your home at Christmas, your family or animals. You could start with the lettering and develop a design with it.

You need to consider the size, the size of envelope and method of reproduction as this will influence your design. The need for careful preparation is reinforced when you realise the numbers in which your card will be produced. Repetition of mistakes or carelessness is embarrassing!

Happy Christmas
Love from Hatty, Philip and Samuel

(*Top*) Christmas card printed on both sides by a professional printer using off-set litho.
(*Centre and bottom*) Free-standing Christmas card cut out from red card.
Folded into a triptych by the printers but the shapes cut out by hand with scissors.

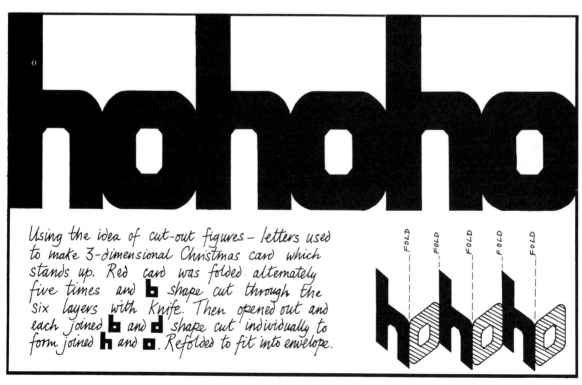

Using the idea of cut-out figures – letters used to make 3-dimensional Christmas card which stands up. Red card was folded alternately five times and **b** shape cut through the six layers with knife. Then opened out and each joined **b** and **d** shape cut individually to form joined **h** and **■**. Refolded to fit into envelope.

FOLD   FOLD   FOLD   FOLD   FOLD

86

Cards for Special Occasions

Birthday cards, congratulations and anniversary cards are more likely to be a one-off job. This gives you plenty of scope for working in a variety of sizes and colours.

Invitations

There is a great boom in the variety and supply of invitation cards for every occasion. You can make your own and these will be even more personal. The amount of decoration will depend on the purpose but the information must be clearly set out. You will not want people turning up on the wrong day nor to upset the bridegroom's family by spelling his name incorrectly! Start by writing out the essential information and then think about the design.

Personal Stationery

Letter-writing has featured quite prominently in this book. The problem of setting out the address could be solved once and for all if you design your own letter headings and maybe a card or notelet to go with it. If you draw well you could include a drawing of your house. You may prefer to design a personal logo or monogram using the initials of your name. The relationship of the drawing or logo to the writing is all-important and both should relate to the shape of the page. For a trial run, you could use photocopying for reproduction before having it printed professionally. A reduction in size or a rearrangement can be made to make this suitable for personal cards, notelets, a compliments slip or a business card.

Brochures

Having ventured as far as letter headings and personal stationery, if you are in business, you may consider producing your own brochure. This is not as daunting as it may seem, it just takes longer and much more thought. Most of the thinking is in compiling the information, putting it in a logical order and then setting it out to look attractive. You may need drawings or photographs for illustration and a map for guidance and these have to be related to the writing. Understanding the alternative methods of printing and knowing how to present your work is essential to the success of producing your own brochure.

Magazines and Books

Producing four sides for a brochure may seem to be ambitious. You could be more so and consider compiling a magazine or book. Many people write poetry, want to write their family history or personal reminiscences, or write stories for children and know that the chances of having their work published are remote. If you are prepared to do the work involved, a very limited edition could be produced by photocopying. Even employing the services of a professional printer is not unreasonable when you provide all the artwork ready for printing. However, it would be wise to get an estimate before you take such a step.

Similarly, magazines for local organisations can be produced, although the cost per copy for a small number may prohibit this. You should do careful estimates before you start. What is good about producing a group magazine and having it photocopied is that you can make use of a wide variety of talents. You could use drawings, handwriting and lettering skills and even accept advertising to help pay for the printing. But, all this depends upon you, as editor, knowing and stating the size to be worked to, doing the costing and being prepared to

TERRACOTTA
Glenside North
Pinchbeck
Spalding
Lincs. PE11 3SD.

Tel. Pinchbeck Bars (077587) 509

10th March 1985

Dear Carole,
    I have now

TERRACOTTA

Helen Lawrence
Terracotta
Glenside North
Pinchbeck
Spalding
Lincs. PE11 3SD.

ART WORKSHOP

Classes for all levels of experience - All ages over 9yrs.
Painting · Drawing · Printing · Ceramics · Sculpture ·

☎ Pinchbeck Bars (077587) 509

TERRA COTT
Glenside Nort
Pinchbeck
Spalding PE11

Tel. Pinchbeck Bars (077

Mrs. W. Wheiser
#247
6th Avenue East
Braceberg
Ontario

Personal stationery: (*Top*) Letter heading on A4. (*Right*) Business card. (*Left*) Folded card A6 or notelet. (*Bottom*) Envelope.

A6-size brochure produced by photocopying. Art work pasted up on an A3 sheet, reduced to A4, printed on both sides and then the two copies are separated by cutting lengthways.

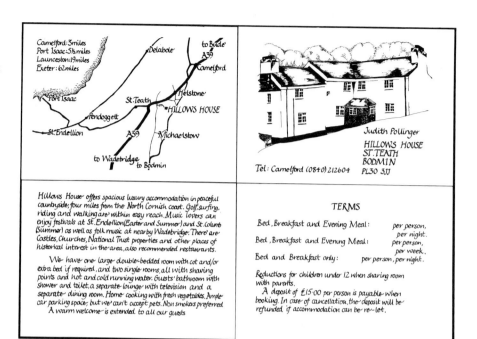

produce the work suitable for printing. In doing your own book you only have yourself to organise but taking on the production of a magazine means giving the right instructions to all contributors.

Several points related to the printing apply to both books and magazines:

- Check the sizes that can be done by photocopying.
- Draw up a guide sheet for the size you have chosen.
- All work done should conform to the outer margins of the guide sheet.

When all the work has been completed, it has to be pasted up on 'same-size' sheets and assembled in the right order. There are three ways of doing this:

- To print the work on one side only and staple the sheets together, or punch holes on the left hand side and put the work in a folder. Alternatively, the assembled sheets can be gripped together with a plastic spine clip which can be bought quite cheaply at a stationer's. More sophisticated folders can be bought for a special job. Also, you could consider mounting the copies on better, or coloured, paper.
- To economise you may want to print on both sides of the paper. Again, using a single sheet which will be fixed on the left hand margin, have your master copies in order, 1, 3, 5, 7, 9 and print these in the numbers required. Turn them over and print pages 2, 4, 6, 8, 10 on the back.

WESTERN CONTACT

Pre-School
Playgroups Association

NEWSLETTER

19

This is a layout for a Playgroup Magazine. For the cover children's drawings were reduced by photocopy & the title letters were cut out as the result seemed more in sympathy with the childrens work. The whole was pasted up at A4, and reduced by photocopy. Contributions for the inside pages were provided by members of the Association ~ a mixture of illustration, typescript and clear handwriting to provide liveliness and emphasis.

...her Frolic
...beautiful
...shows
...jelly
...run, the
...during
...s. The
...ittee
...ends for
...Julie
... term.
... great
...rived on
the last morning of term to see her presented
with a set of wine glasses and two bottles of
wine by Martin Marote, one of the playgroup
children. Everybody connected with the playgroup
wishes Julie and Peter all the best in their
new home, and welcome Jill Brown in her new role
as Supervisor. Jill has been working in the
Playgroup and everyone hopes she will enjoy her
new job.

A very big thank you to all those who contributed an article. I hope that most of you will be encouraged/ enraged/ enticed to put pen to paper for the next edition.

FOLD. NOT
COMFORTA...
CHILDREN...
A SIMPLIFI...
CANDLE, C...
AND USING...
ASSORTED P...
HELP EACH...
HIS OR HER...
BELOVED GR...
WHOEVER TH...
BE WRITTEN...
OR THE CHI...

TINTAGEL PRE-SCHOOL PLAYGROUP

COME TO OUR 'CAROLS FOR EVERYONE' SERVICE
COME TO OUR 'CAROLS FOR EVERYONE' SERVICE
ON WEDNESDAY 17th DECEMBER, STARTING
AT 7pm IN TINTAGEL SOCIAL HALL WITH
THE ST BREWARD SILVER BAND —
TICKETS ARE 50p FOR ADULTS, AND 25p
FOR CHILDREN OVER 5 (UNDER 5's FREE)
TICKETS INCLUDE A SAVOURY SUPPER
AN ENJOYABLE EVENING GUARANTEED FOR ALL

Cover and four pages for a playgroup magazine. Twenty-four pages, plus cover to be produced on both sides of A4 sheets, assembled in the correct order and stapled together using a long-arm stapler.

- To print a double page to make a book that can be folded in half and stapled in the middle. Ten or twelve such pages are the most that can be stapled together comfortably but this will give you a 48 page booklet.

Pasting up and the order of printing is more complicated. First of all, have each page on a separate sheet. Assume there are 24 pages, plus covers. You will need 14 double page sheets for mounting the pages.

Pasting up is done like this:

First print run		Turn over sheets for second run	
Back cover	Front cover	Inside front	Inside Back
24	1	2	23
22	3	4	21
20	5	6	19
18	7	8	17
16	9	10	15
14	11	12	13

Fold the sheets separately, assemble them in the right order and use a long-arm stapler to staple them in the middle.

Some photocopy operators may consider this job to be an unreasonable demand on their services. Ask first and assure them that you will have all your work in order. Certainly, anything more complicated will have to be taken to a professional printer. However, producing your own book or magazine, albeit a time consuming task, is worthwhile and personally rewarding.

Lettercutting in
Wood, Slate and
Stone
After all this, it may be a relief to use your lettering skills on a different material. If you have had some experience of working in wood, slate or stone you could work on these to produce house names, memorials or a sundial.

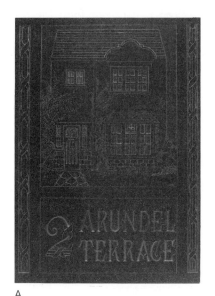

A

B

C

F

D

E

Lettering in wood and
slate.

A Arundel Terrace: nameplate cut in Delabole slate;   B Jewellery box: pattern and
monogram carved in mahogany;   C HCH: monogram carved in oak to be placed at the
house entrance;   D Penwarnick: house name cut in Delabole Slate;   E Stonecarving:
business plate cut in Delabole Slate;   F Letter samples: cut in oak.

THE JOY OF GOOD WRITING

which all can achieve

REQUIRES

PATIENCE

not to expect too much too soon

DETERMINATION

not to give up
when progress seems slow

DILIGENCE

to work with steady purpose

PLEASURE

in the work
exasperation and low spirits
are poor companions

AND A

GOOD GUIDE

to show the way.

This book is a guide through the informal "hand writing" stage.
Should you wish to progress further, into formal Calligraphy, there
are short courses arranged by the Society of Scribes and Illuminators
% British Crafts Centre, 43 Earlham Street, London WC2H 9LD.
Calligraphy books are available in most libraries and book shops.

WENDY SELBY

Index